D1453803

CONTENTS

ABOUT THE AUTHOR.

Ross Turner is a lifelong entrepreneur, and an expert in the media, marketing, and branding industry. He has over a decade of hands-on experience managing and consulting on international marketing campaigns for large corporations, churches, politicians, and public figures.

In addition to being a respected expert in marketing, Ross has been a passionate follower of Christ his entire life. He is the owner and CEO of Vibrant Agency, one of the fastest growing graphic design, web development, and video design agencies in the world for Christian organizations. His team works directly with many prominent international ministries to grow their influence and online presence.

Ross lives with his wife and two children on California's central coast. They are deeply involved in their local church and love serving in ministries everywhere they can.

FOREW

As the Executive Director for the Association of Related Churches (ARC), I get to personally consult with thousands of pastors and church planters all around the world. One of the topics that frequently comes up in our conferences and private coaching sessions is the topic of marketing and advertising. It is a tool that many of us need to sharpen. Many pastors feel completely overwhelmed when trying to learn how to use digital marketing to help grow their church. It can be difficult to know if you are doing advertising and marketing the right way, especially when it comes to spending your resources on ads.

That is why this book is so crucial for church leaders. The topics covered in this book will give church leaders incredibly valuable knowledge. When done right, marketing can be one of the key factors in driving first-time visitors to your church. Ross and his team have developed a unique marketing strategy that churches can benefit from. When you understand how to use a marketing funnel, you will start to see results like you never have before with marketing.

ORD

At ARC we teach classes and training sessions about digital marketing, but we don't have the time to dive as deeply as we would like. I have been hoping for a resource like this to come out for churches, and provide the in-depth training that pastors and church leaders need.

I truly hope that you take the time to understand the principles outlined in this book, and use your newfound skills to reach the lost.

Dino Rizzo
Executive Director, ARC

SECRET ONE

YOU HAVE TO GET YOUR MIND RIGHT.

YOU HAVE TO GET YOUR MIND RIGHT.

WE ARE A CHURCH, NOT A BUSINESS.
WE DON'T REALLY NEED TO CHANGE EVERYTHING, DO WE?

Every year, I speak with hundreds of church leaders all over the world who want to reach more people in their local community with the Gospel. They know the marketing tools are out there, but they don't know the first thing about how to use them. And with the demanding and busy lifestyle of ministry, church leaders don't have the time to teach themselves how to market their church. Maybe this sounds like you?

Marketing, advertising, sales funnels—these are all secular business terms. Large corporations and advertising agencies have spent countless hours studying exactly what works to compel someone to make a purchasing decision. I should know; I was one of them. I am the CEO and founder of Vibrant Agency, an international church media company. However, when I first started, I was working on the branding, online marketing, and sales funnels of corporate businesses. We quickly rose to be a national competitor in our industry using the exact principles outlined in this book, and now you get to put them to work for your church. Those of us who are experienced in this industry can instantly tell when an ad is done by a professional, and when it is not. We know what will work, and what will not. In marketing, there are principles that are game changers, and once you understand them, your church growth will never look the same.

More often than I want to admit, I get hate comments online from cranky Christians telling me that it is heresy to talk about marketing for churches. Just take a look at some of the comments I get on Facebook. However, what these cranky Christians don't understand is that in the days that we are living in, marketing is a vital component to reaching others for the Gospel. The problem is, churches are getting it all wrong. I cannot tell you how many times I have seen a church ad on social media or Google that is—simply put—a disaster. It pains me to see churches wasting their often limited resources on advertising campaigns that simply won't work. And don't even get me started on some of the branding I see. **Side note—please stop downloading stock logo icons and slapping your church's name on it.**

GET YOUR MIND RIGHT.

It is time to start understanding that using every method possible to reach people is a mandate. If you are being passive and just hoping that people happen to wander through your sanctuary doors, I argue that you are not being faithful. As a church leader, your motive is obviously different than a business owner. However, the very principles and strategies that we use in the secular world to reach new customers are the same principles that can be used to reach people for Jesus. Instead of using advertising to make money, you want to use it to win your city for Christ. This is what we are called to do. And in this book, I am going to teach you exactly how to do it. Everything my agency has learned over the past decade is now yours.

Most people who enter into vocational ministry do not have experience in branding or marketing. Obviously. And eventually they realize that it is important, so they try and figure it out on the fly. When they do it the wrong way, they end up wasting their resources on marketing campaigns that produce very little results. Does this sound like anyone you know?

You don't have to wait for people to walk through your doors to impact them. Go meet them right where they are.

It was Jesus himself who used parallels to secular business methods when he was instructing his disciples. In Matthew chapter ten, he instructs them to go from city to city telling people the good news. Tradesmen would travel from city to city to sell their goods and livestock, but Jesus had the disciples do this same thing for the Gospel. It was the most effective way to spread the news. The motive changed, but the method was similar.

Jesus also used an analogy of fishing to help us understand how to reach new people. In Matthew chapter four, Jesus looked out on the water and saw Peter and Andrew hard at work as fishermen. Then Jesus told them to follow him and to become fishers of men. Peter and Andrew stopped putting all of their work into building their fishing business, then used what they had learned in fishing to reach people for Christ. They knew that being a fisher of men meant being active. In fishing, you don't wait for fish to jump in the boat, but you cast your net to where the fish already are. You go to them.

Jesus still wants us to be fishers of men, but times and technologies have since changed, so we can now cast our nets in a different way. Maybe you feel uncertain of how to go about this whole marketing thing, but Peter and Andrew probably felt the same way the first time they were on a fishing boat. They had to have someone first teach them how to be great fishermen; it didn't just happen. They were trained. In this book, I am going to train you how to fish for souls using marketing and advertising. Everything I have learned about sales behavior, digital marketing, and advertising, I am giving to you in this book. It is my prayer that this information will be the catalyst that will inspire you to create the ultimate funnel that helps change lives in your city.

You have to change your mindset about marketing. It is a vital part of our call to go into all the world and spread the Gospel.

SECRET TWO

POOR FOUNDATIONS YIELD POOR RESULTS.

FOUNDATIONS OVERVIEW

There is a tool that you can use to continuously grow your church with new people, and it is called the funnel. But before I give you the rundown on the funnel and you become a genius at marketing your church, there are some foundational pieces that you really need to get right. You may remember a certain teaching about building your house upon a firm foundation. The same applies to your marketing.

Let's do a deep dive on your marketing foundations. Here is a hard truth: if your church doesn't have the topics in this chapter dialed in—it doesn't matter how good your marketing is—your church won't have long-term, sustainable growth.

However, if you get the foundations described in this chapter right, there is a chance that your church could grow in numbers over the long haul, even without doing any marketing or advertising at all. That's how important these foundations are. The only thing that marketing and advertising will do is make growth happen more quickly. Countless businesses and ministries have contacted our team to help reach new numerical growth goals, and the very first thing we do is analyze the foundations. I am never surprised to hear when a church has done a lot of marketing and advertising with little to no results, because it almost always means that their marketing and branding isn't built on a firm foundation.

It is easy to change your marketing. It is nearly impossible to change your reputation. Good news: nothing is impossible with God. If you focus on the foundational principles of branding and culture, then add the marketing funnel, you will see the fruits that you have been wanting to see. It is hard to go back to the start, but it is worth it!

In this chapter we are going to discuss how to build firm foundations by:

1. Defining your target audience.
2. Setting specific goals.
3. Creating your culture.
4. Celebrating invites.
5. Embracing being digital.
6. Learning your personality.

Through this foundation, your community will learn who and what your church is about. The marketing only helps get the word out.

Pro Tip - Consider having your team read this chapter with you and give their input on your ministry's foundations. Make it a team collaboration to get an honest evaluation of the strengths and weaknesses of what you are trying to build on.

DEFINE YOUR TARGET AUDIENCE.

JESUS LOVES EVERYONE, SO DON'T WE WANT TO TARGET EVERYONE WITH OUR MARKETING?

Every single person in your city, within a fifty-mile radius…
that's your target audience. Right? If that is your mindset, you
have an uphill battle in front of you. Don't get me wrong, you
certainly want to see every man, woman, and child come to
know Jesus through your church. As Christians, we love everyone! But here is the crazy truth: **to reach more people, focus
on fewer people.** Your church is going to make a much deeper
impact on your community if you tailor the entire experience
to a specific demographic. It seems counterintuitive, I know.
Keep reading.

When I started my first marketing company I had no in-
tention of making it an agency specifically for ministries. Sure,
I wanted to help churches, but I also wanted to have clients in
numerous other industries. The more business types that we
would serve, the bigger our company would be. *So I thought.* Initially I designed our website and our marketing to showcase the
great pricing and offers we had, but I never specified what kind
of industry we specialized in. I didn't want to exclude anyone.

We were a marketing agency for any and all businesses.

But unfortunately our marketing was totally failing. I was confused as to why very few people were clicking on our ads, and we were barely getting any sales from our website. It was completely deflating. Why couldn't I get clients when our prices were cheaper than our competitors, and our service was better? What the heck?

After some prayer and reflection, I felt that God had put a passion in my heart to help churches. I really didn't have lasting fulfillment helping the kinds of businesses that I had been serving, so maybe God was leading me into a new thing. I realized that I was tired of spending all of my time helping businesses that I had no passion for. However, the church is something that excites me—it's something I do have a passion for. In the past, I had been on staff at a few churches, and both my wife and I grew up in ministry. Ministry has always been our number one thing, so the idea of being able to put everything I've learned about marketing into helping churches and being a resource for church leaders sounded incredible! But to be honest, I genuinely felt that it was too niche of a market to be sustainable for a business. I thought that there wouldn't be enough clients for me to grow a successful agency.

But I went for it. I launched our new entity called Vibrant Agency and made it 100% focused on exclusively serving the marketing and media needs of churches. I stayed up all night (quite literally) and put together our whole website and set up our social media profiles. By dawn, Vibrant Agency was officially a full-service media and marketing agency for churches, and only for churches. The next day, I opened my computer and launched three different Instagram and Facebook ads exclusively for pastors. **It felt so weird having such a small niche audience. I really didn't think it would work.** I was in for a huge shock.

To my amazement I was getting a hundred times the amount of leads, web traffic, and conversions than I was just two days before. I signed on our first church in less than one week of this new launch. **Even though our ads targeted fewer people, we grew exponentially.**

Fast forward six years later. As of 2020, we are now one of the nation's leading marketing agencies for churches. How cool is that? Although I greatly reduced the number of people in the target audience I was advertising to, our marketing was now much more effective. Why is that? It's because we were now the specialist to that niche audience. Our target audience knew we were the right fit for them. We spoke the language of pastors and church leaders, and they felt more comfortable partnering with us because we had their trust. We were their people.

Sometimes you have to become smaller in order to get bigger.

This story goes to show that **highly defining your target audience does not mean fewer people, it means more.** When you define the exact type of person that you want to tailor your church's experience for, you are much more likely for that person to feel like you "get" them. They will be proud to be a part of your church, because they feel like they belong. You are their people. Take the plunge and make your whole strategy based on one specific type of person, and become the best for them. **You can't be the best for everyone; just be the very best for one demographic.**

But wait, there is good news. Even though you focus on one demographic, that doesn't mean you will only reach that one person type. Other demographics will also be served by and attracted to your church. I am constantly amazed by how many people don't fit into our cultural norms. I see people that don't fit certain stereotypes—wearing brands, attending events, or watching shows that I would have never guessed that they would like. You don't have to worry that your church will end up only serving a specific type of person, or that everyone else will feel out of place. This is just about making your marketing specific. You will still have a well-rounded congregation, and people will still feel like they belong, even if they are outside of your defined target audience. Don't be all things to all people, but find who you truly are and go all in with that.

Here are a few examples of a well-defined target audience:
- Young couples with children under ten years old
- Men between the ages of twenty-one and thirty who have a worldly past
- Established professionals in their forties
- Local college-aged students

You need to be prayerful and strategic when deciding who your target audience is. There must be a combination of natural intuition and seeking God's leading. Sometimes your location makes the choice easier for you. If you live in a college town filled with hip twenty-three-year-olds, that might be who you target. Maybe your area is filled with business professionals or young families. Take your natural demographics into consideration, pray about it, and define your target audience.

 If you define, your numbers will climb. (You like that?)

Pro Tip - Whoever you decide is your target audience, use photos of that demographic on your website and social media feed as much as possible.

SET SPECIFIC GOALS.

MORE PEOPLE, THAT'S THE GOAL. PRETTY SIMPLE, RIGHT?

If you want to succeed, you need to know exactly what success means for your church. **Without clearly-defined and measurable goals, it will be difficult to know if your marketing is working.**

This is not a book on goal setting, but I want to briefly touch on how to set specific goals for tracking numerical church growth. Using the funnel to grow your ministry is a long game, and is not easily measured using short-term metrics. However, there are benchmarks that you should focus on as you monitor your progress.

There are three steps for setting and achieving specific goals within your marketing:
1. Define the growth goal.
2. Track your progress.
3. Adjust the funnel to achieve success.

- **Define the growth goal.**
  The first thing to do is define what your specific goal is, and then reverse engineer it. Your goal may be to increase the weekend service attendance by 15% each year. Or your goal

might be to increase your engagement and following on social media. Maybe your goal is to increase your livestream views or to increase the global reach of your ministry, reaching beyond your local community. Each of these goals will have their own unique way of measuring and tracking progress. For the purpose of this section, we are going to focus on the specific goal of increasing weekend service attendance. Churches should define a growth percentage for the year rather than a monthly goal.

As everyone in ministry knows, attendance varies greatly from season to season. Summer is traditionally lower than the fall. Easter is high, spring break is low…you know how it goes. With weekend church attendance, the biggest goal that you should focus on is the year-to-year growth percentage. Because of the variation of seasons, weather, and local events, you shouldn't put too much stock in month-by-month numbers. Quarterly reports are a much better way to track your progress and help you know if you should adjust your marketing to hit your yearly goal. But you have to have a specific percentage goal first. Once you have a specific yearly percentage goal, how do you know if you are growing at the right pace to meet your goal?

- ## Track your progress.
  In order to really track your progress, be sure that you have accurate attendance numbers for each service. It should be someone's job to take a head count during each service, and further break it down by first-time guests, kids' ministry, youth ministry, and main service attendance. Log the number of salvations each week so you have something to celebrate later on. Each week, this person should put these numbers into a spreadsheet or database. Although this may seem tedious, these numbers are going to be crucial moving forward in your marketing decisions. You have to know if you need to make any

adjustments to your advertising budget to help hit your goals.

It will be very important to have a strong first-time guest system in place at your church. You don't want to be the kind of church that gets a lot of first-time guests but doesn't keep them. A common belief is that it takes someone four services in a row for them to stick. So you need to have a strong next-step plan for new guests that helps keep them engaged for the first four weeks. You want to make sure that your emphasis is a great balance between trying to gain first-time guests, and also making sure to fully retain the visitors you have.

Be sure to offer an awesome gift to all first-time visitors. The gift is strategic because it helps get data and contact information, which you need for your follow-up plan. Make it a great gift, and be creative with it. Some churches give hoodies, hats, or coffee mugs. These are great! You can consider giving out small gift cards, or even just a candy bar will do the trick when you're on a budget.

While you're connecting with first-time guests, ask them where they first found out about the church. This is incredibly helpful! Statistics say that it takes at least seven impressions before someone takes action on an advertising campaign. Most of the time, new visitors will have had multiple "touches" of your church before they take action. Some people will first see you on social media, and then maybe hear about you at work, and then see some Facebook ads, then finally they will be invited by someone personally. The hope is that they will see your church all over the place. If your first-time guest says that the reason they came is because they were invited by a friend, it is likely that they said "yes" not just because of the invitation, but also because they have been seeing marketing on other platforms as well. It takes more than an ad or a mailer. **When everything works together, that is when the magic happens.**

This is why marketing is a long game, and is best measured from a year-to-year metric. It takes a lot of touches before a decision happens.

- ## Adjust the funnel.

What should you do if you get through the first two quarters of the year and you are behind the pace of your annual growth goal? **This is the beauty of the funnel—it is scalable.** Once you understand the funnel, you will know how to adjust it to better meet your goals. The funnel will show you how many advertising dollars it costs to get one new guest, and you can increase or decrease the marketing budget to achieve your annual goal. If you are needing to boost your growth by an additional ten guests per weekend, you can increase your budget and speed up your funnel. However, if you are growing rapidly, you can slow down the funnel if you want. This does actually happen! We recently had a church in Ohio ask us to stop running the funnel ads because they were growing too quickly, and they needed to slow down the pace.

Whether you have a large marketing budget or nearly no budget at all, you can still use the funnel to attract new guests, but you will only know to make adjustments if you diligently track your numbers. If your goals are not specific and measurable, then you won't know if the marketing is working.

Set specific goals. Measure your progress. You'll thank me later.

Pro Tip - If your first-time guest gift is really great, people will be willing to give you their contact information. Ask them if they saw your ads on social media and have an intern or volunteer follow up with them by sending a direct message inviting them to an upcoming event. If the relationship started online, they might feel comfortable taking next steps that way too.

CREATE YOUR CULTURE.

AT OUR CHURCH, WE'RE DIFFERENT. NOBODY ELSE SAYS THAT, DO THEY?

We've talked about setting strategic goals, and how valuable it is. Part of understanding how to set your goals is to know what the culture of your church really is. What are the benefits of being unique and different as a church? Every church I have consulted says they are "different," and in many subtle ways they certainly are, but being unique and different only helps if it has an intentional strategy behind it.

A church on a specific mission is attractive. People don't want to come to church just to be spiritually fed, but they want to be a part of something big. Your church will become known in the community for something, and it is really hard to change that perspective once it is developed. How people feel about your church is what the industry calls your brand. I'm not talking about your logo, I am talking about your brand—who people perceive you to be.

There is good news. You can control the narrative if you are careful.

You need to pick a specific purpose. Of course all churches have the same big-picture goals. At least they should. We all want to see people give their lives to Jesus, and be changed by the Gospel. That's what we want. We are not talking about changing that part. The purpose and cultural uniqueness that you should focus on within your church is much more subtle.

Most people who have been touched and changed by Jesus want to give back. They want to make an impact on others. If your church has a special mission, it helps to establish your culture and your community perspective. People usually don't become deeply rooted in a church simply because they enjoy the worship or the teaching. They stay when they believe in the mission of the church, and they feel like they are a part of the culture. They want to be proud to be a part of your church, and this happens when you intentionally establish your culture. **A joint mission builds culture.**

Let me break it down by giving you some examples. It will be tempting to say that you want to have all of these missions, but try and find a specific one. A clearly-defined mission helps people buy in. Certainly you can serve and minister in all of these areas, but have just one of these focus points be the primary ministry. Trust me when I say, you want to narrow your focus to one primary mission. This is how to build a uniform culture.

Here are some examples of key missions that help build the culture in your church:

Focus on the poor and homeless.

Deciding that your church is going to put extra emphasis on the poor and homeless is a great way to help the community and establish a culture that people can really get behind. Creating ministries to help shelter the homeless and programs to help get them back on their feet is a great idea. You could buy buses and start shuttling in people to your services each Sunday from areas of town that have a large homeless population. Sometimes having special offerings where people can give to a specific homeless shelter is a great idea too. These are all things that people get excited about and help them know what your church stands for. If this is on your heart, make it a special point of emphasis for your church, and people will be eager to make a difference.

- ## Focus on your community.

Being a church that is in love with your city and local community is a great way to get people to really connect. Having a presence at local farmers' markets, city-wide events, rallies, and festivals are some great ways to build this culture. Most people love where they live and have a heart to help improve their city and reach the lives of the people who live there. You could have part of your tagline be something like "We Love San Diego" or make frequent references to your city on social media. To be a part of a church that pours into their community can really mean a lot to people. Many churches will spend an entire week, or even month, putting on "serve days" where the church goes into the community to show love to their city. This builds culture in a strong and deep way. If this is your focus point, people should know without a doubt that joining your church means they are going to be asked to give back to the community in some way. Through your church, your community will be impacted, and people will feel deeply fulfilled.

- ## Focus on families.

Having a church that has a special emphasis on a strong family life can be one of the healthiest missions possible. Having frequent message series revolving around marriage, parenting, and family dynamics helps build a culture that people can really embrace. Make this your church's special mission by putting your resources into the kids and youth areas of your facility. Make it great. Put on special events for kids and teens, and even date nights for couples. When your church focuses on being the church for families, you will let first-time guests know that they are making a wise move for their family if they join your church. People will know that your church is a place that grows healthy families.

- ## Focus on art & creativity.

This one might surprise you to be on this list. It doesn't seem as altruistic and spiritual as the others, and I get that. Some of the largest and most globally influential churches that I have worked with have services that are incredibly artistic, and creativity is celebrated. If I started listing them, you would instantly know who I was talking about. The music is unique and really high quality. The decor of the church is beautiful and unlike traditional churches. The graphics and videos are also so unique and compelling. If your church has a celebration of a creative culture, you will attract like-minded people. People who come to your church will know that it is a great place for them to express themselves.

This list is not in any way meant to be an exhaustive list, and there are probably a hundred different focus missions that you could choose. But it is important to think about your community and what matters to them. Whatever God has built your church to be, that is what your unique culture should be. **Be about something, or you are about nothing.**

All of these areas are great and are needed, and your church can still serve multiple missions, but when you choose one specific area to be your key focus point, you will see a culture start to develop. It takes intentionality to create a culture within your church, and once that catches on, it will become known in the community as well.

Decide what you are known for, or it will be decided for you. Or worse, you won't be known for anything.

Pro Tip - Redo your tagline to include what your mission is all about.

LEARN YOUR PERSONALITY.

HOW MUCH DOES THE PASTOR'S PERSONALITY ACTUALLY AFFECT OUR CULTURE?

What people think of your church is deeply tied to what they think of the lead pastor. In fact, it is not often that churches fully survive a change of lead pastors, because the culture of the church is so closely tied to that one person. **People will always trust the person more than they will trust the logo.** It's part of your job, if you're the lead pastor, to work on your personality, because it affects your ability to reach new people.

It is hard to follow a leader who is not likable. Obviously, right? Many pastors whom we have worked with want to create working systems, marketing campaigns, and a Sunday experience that all flow well together, but it just doesn't seem to catch on. Why not? If these same systems work for many others, why does it not work for them? The bailout answer is to blame it on your city and local culture. But sometimes there is a bigger problem, and it is the leadership.

If your church is new or small, you do not have the luxury of hiding behind systems. In smaller churches, almost everyone in the church will need a personal connection to the pastor at some level. Simply put, if you are the lead pastor, your church members have to like you personally before they are going to receive from you spiritually. You need to build up the relationship equity with people, which takes work.

You may ask, why is this relevant in a book about church marketing? It is because everything works together, whether you realize it or not. As a pastor, you should think of it like this: a lot of the people who follow your church's Instagram account, will then follow your personal account as well. In fact, many of the posts on your personal profile will actually get more engagement than the posts on the church's profile. This is because people long to know you personally. By being a lead pastor, you have given up the right to be antisocial, at least in the beginning phases of your church.

The next time you are thinking about content to put out on social media, don't just think in terms of posting on the church's profile. There should be content also coming directly from your personal account. And if you don't want to film videos because you are uncomfortable in front of a camera, then you might be in the wrong job. I implore you to not just work on marketing systems and strategies, but to work on yourself. I know it will be hard for some of you who are not naturally social, or are highly introverted. But get in the trenches and be involved in people's lives. Go to birthday parties with other families. Have people over to your house for barbecues. Go to kids' baseball games. Have coffee with someone, and be real about life. Be vulnerable. Be a leader not just behind a desk, but be a friend to as many people as you can.

People have to know you, and people have to like you. It is part of the job of expanding the influence and reach of your church. It is part of building your culture and your brand.

Pro Tip - Block off two times per week to meet with families from your church for coffee or some social activity. If it is on the calendar, it will be more likely to happen.

CELEBRATE INVITES.

PEOPLE KNOW THAT THEY SHOULD INVITE OTHERS TO CHURCH. DON'T THEY?

You can have all of the marketing in the world, get the culture right, and even have the best sermons and the most lovable pastor ever, but until your people start inviting their friends, co-workers, and family to church, you will be disappointed at the pace of your church growth. There is nothing like good, old-fashioned word of mouth to foster growth, and to do that, you need invites.

You need to make a big deal about invites. **You need to celebrate invites.** You even need to preach about the value of invites. It really is that important. For some reason, people don't remember to invite people unless they are asked. So ask. And then ask again. Your whole church should know that they are in this to reach people, and inviting people is a huge part of growing God's Kingdom.

There are many ways that you can build a precedent that emphasizes inviting people. You should treat first-time guests like royalty. Talk to them, introduce them to people, have someone take them out to lunch. Make sure your church members know that each guest should feel welcomed, celebrated, and comfortable. This makes the guest have a pleasant experience in what normally might be an uncomfortable one. But even more importantly, this also sets a standard that makes members comfortable and confident in bringing their guests to church. If they know that their guests are going to be treated like royalty, they will want to invite people.

Since you are tracking your numbers, share these victories with the congregation. Every month you should share the great news of how many new people came to the church. Celebrate even more when you follow it up with how many of them were invited by a friend! Make it exciting. Positive reinforcement will cause an increase in your invite numbers over the long haul.

If you celebrate the invites, the invites will increase.

Pro Tip - Make a quarterly video of a family whose lives were changed once they started coming to your church. And make sure that the person who invited them for the first time is a part of the video so others can see how big of an impact they can make in the church and in people's lives.

EMBRACE BEING DIGITAL.

I HATE IT WHEN PEOPLE STAY HOME TO WATCH OUR LIVESTREAM, SHOULDN'T THEY JUST COME TO A SERVICE?

Before social media and iPhones came around, your church could simply put all the focus on having an awesome Sunday service. If someone missed it, bummer for them. But even though inviting guests and attending church on-campus is great, times have changed, and church attendance looks differently than it used to. These are exciting times!

Like it or not, people are connecting with their "home church" differently now. You should stop trying to fight it. Now more than ever, people are getting spiritually fed by podcasts, YouTube messages, and social media content. Not just on Sunday mornings. **And maybe that's ok.** ⟵

This could be an advantage for your church, not a problem.

Wait, what? You might be thinking, I want people to show up on Sundays, and instead they are staying home and watching our livestream. This is not what we wanted. Our real church family are those who come in person.

I get it, but you are dead wrong. The local church is never going away, but the way you deliver your message needs to adapt. **Adapting isn't compromising. Adapting is smart.** Jesus wasn't preaching on a stage with an LED wall behind him, with the perfect amount of haze in the air. We adapted to current technologies, and now we use all of the technology we can in church. It is not bad, it is great! Why then are we so often resistant to change?

As I write this book, our planet has been completely turned upside down. Almost every restaurant, school, and even church has been mandated by the government to temporarily close its doors. I am writing this chapter in the middle of the COVID-19 pandemic that has changed our world—a virus so contagious that we have been forced to have church exclusively online, work from home every day, and parents have now stepped into the world of homeschooling. And worst of all, it happened right before Easter. As terrible as this situation has been, I know there are going to be some lasting impacts for the church. For the first time, we are going to fully focus on doing ministry online. Our primary ministry is going to happen with cameras and phones. I believe this season is going to be a catalyst that changes us and helps us realize that church is much more than a building.

In the secular business world, the companies that make it the easiest to buy their products, win. The path of least resistance will always succeed in the end. Would you rather spend two hours in Walmart buying groceries and home goods, including impulse buys that will break your perfectly planned budget, or would you rather order everything you need from Amazon and have it delivered to your front door? Would people rather get dressed up, drive to church, drop off their kids, and then hear your message, or would it be easier if they could just grab their phones and listen at home?

I know I just made all of you mad, so here is the disclaimer: gathering together as believers is both highly important, and very biblical. Mature Christians get that. **But what about the**

people who are just testing the waters? It is for them that we adapt.
Once someone matures in their faith, they will then understand why we are called to physically gather together. But until then, let's make receiving the Gospel message as easy as possible. Adapt. The value of your church is much deeper than where the person is physically sitting when they listen to your message. It is about the joint mission, the community and relationships, and the gathering of the saints, but it is not doing you any good to be nostalgic about where the people are when they hear your message.

You need to shift your perspective. Your church doesn't just meet on Sundays at a single defined physical location anymore. I believe that God would have you be faithful to reach people with the tools that you have at your disposal during this period in history. There will still be many people who will prefer to come and join the service live on Sundays, and we love that. There will also be many people who prefer to join in the message from the convenience of their homes. Yet these same people will be active participants in Bible studies, outreach events, home gatherings, and more.

The wrong thing to do is to fight it. You will not win. The right thing to do is to embrace this reality, and adapt your strategy. You should be creating videos and message content throughout the week on social media and your website. Not just on Sundays. If convenience is what people need, deliver the Gospel to them right where they are at. Soon, you should be putting your very best stuff online instead of just focusing on the in-person experience.

As an example, I'd like you to think of your church as if you were the executive director of the TV show Saturday Night Live (SNL). It's a pretty raunchy show, so this is not an endorsement…but it is a great analogy. It would be a pretty cool experience to sit in the Saturday Night Live audience and experience the music and entertainment in person. But how many seats are in that studio? Right under two hundred. The whole experience is primarily built as a TV program for the at-home viewer, not the live audience. Even though they only have two hundred seats, their audience can be measured in the millions. If SNL was primarily an in-person show, they would not have nearly the reach that they have now. The directors of SNL tailored the content for the people sitting in their living rooms eating Doritos.

Your church should be thought of in a similar way. Yes the in-person Sunday services should be powerful and a great experience. However, as more and more people get used to being spiritually fed through online channels, your church needs to be producing your best media for those people. This does not replace community and relationships; it simply changes where they consume the message. If you think I am crazy, just go check your livestream stats. Almost all the churches we work with are already experiencing more people online than in person.

Community, relationships, and gatherings will still happen. But your online members should no longer be considered second-class citizens.

Pro Tip - Make a short, candid video that releases on Facebook and Instagram one hour before your service that welcomes viewers and gives an overview of what you are teaching on. If you do this every week, it will remind people to tune in.

SECRET THREE

YOU NEED A FUNNEL.

OVERVIEW OF THE FUNNEL.

SO WHAT IS THIS "FUNNEL" ALL ABOUT?

More than anything else, I am known for my talks on sales funnels and church growth. I know that your church is not a business, so talking about sales and marketing funnels seems really weird. I get that. But you need to understand what the funnel is, and how it is a proven method for reaching new people. This chapter will teach you how to use a marketing and advertising funnel to actually reach new people. **It simply works.**

What is the funnel? In simple terms, it is the course of decision making when someone engages with a new brand. When someone makes a choice to buy something online, try a new restaurant, or go to a church, there is a specific process that they go through. Once you understand this process, you can tailor your marketing to guide people on each step of their journey. The progression is exactly like a funnel. Picture one of those real life funnels where you can pour liquid or sand into a big cone, and it spits it out through a small hole at the bottom. A funnel is wide at the top, and gets progressively smaller until it gets to the bottom. This real life funnel is the analogy for how professional marketing is done. At the top of your funnel, you get your message out to a lot of people who barely know your brand. Then you progressively move them down your marketing funnel until they end up at the bottom and take a precise action.

Each phase of this marketing funnel has a different goal and a different message that you promote. If you can visualize your marketing like a funnel, then you will ask your target audience to take the right steps. You can't go for the big ask with every ad, or your marketing will be flat and ineffective. Your marketing should only be built to progress people to the next phase of the funnel. The goal isn't always a new visitor on Sunday morning, the goal is progress.

To get a visual on the step-by-step process, check out the diagram of the funnel below.

THE FUNNEL

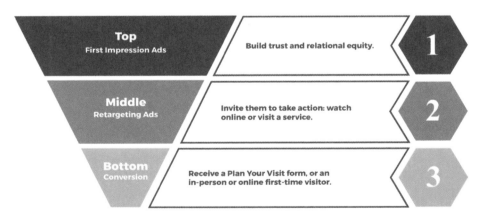

Top First Impression Ads	Build trust and relational equity.	1
Middle Retargeting Ads	Invite them to take action: watch online or visit a service.	2
Bottom Conversion	Receive a Plan Your Visit form, or an in-person or online first-time visitor.	3

In this diagram you can see that people are taken on a journey. The biggest number of people are introduced to your church at the top of the funnel. Next is the middle of the funnel where we ask them to take a next step, and then the conversion, at the bottom of the funnel, is when they come to one of your services or connect online. In the following pages, we are going to discuss the best ways to reach people at the top and the middle of the funnel, and guide them on the journey to a conversion.

To fully understand how the funnel works, you must first understand that people go through a certain process when they make decisions, whether they are aware of it or not. If you want to influence people, then you need to understand them first. **You have to stop trying to go from A to Z in one big leap, but learn to embrace the process.** People don't go from A to Z, they go from A to B… and then B to C…and so on. Likewise, people don't go from ignoring Jesus, to 100% sold-out, on-fire believers in one instant. It is a process.

This is the essence of the funnel. You start on the top, and take people on a journey **one step at a time.** If you will understand and embrace the funnel, it will open your eyes to making decisions with your marketing that are intentional, instead of just blasting ads asking people to come to church. Don't ask people who barely know you to come on a Sunday. You are skipping all the steps.

The goal of marketing is to take people to the next step in the funnel. That's it. If done correctly, you will see genuine fruits of your marketing. If done wrongly, you will likely spend a lot of hours—and dollars—without seeing results.

In traditional e-commerce business, digital marketers are obsessed with perfecting the marketing funnel. Let's first discuss how this funnel works in the corporate world, then zoom in and talk about how a marketing funnel works in the church world. The top of the funnel is where people are first introduced to your product or offer. This is generally where the masses first see a commercial or an advertisement promoting a product. Following that, there are a set of specific steps involved in the buying process. What steps do we want people to take? You might decide you want them to first see an offer for a free resource, then you want them to visit your website, then perhaps you want to follow up with a different ad for the next step, and finally you call them…you get it. It doesn't have to be this specific formula, because each company has its own funnel that it uses to get new customers.

Often the audience is presented with a promotion at the top of the funnel, and those who are interested will move on to the next layer in the funnel. This is where they are sent to a specific page on a website, and are presented with the details of an offer. From there, it is up to the consumer whether they make a purchase or not.

Some companies have a simple three-step funnel, such as offer/website/purchase, but some companies have an extensive multi-step sales funnel that is much more elaborate. However, the step-by-step concept is still the same—regardless of how many steps are in the process—and it applies to your church in more ways than you can imagine.

To define what specific steps you want people to take when entering your church marketing funnel, you first must decide what the end goal is. You would probably agree with me that the most effective way of introducing Jesus to people is by having them come to a service and experience him for themselves or, when appropriate, watch a livestream right then while the service is happening. Most churches have an opportunity somewhere in the service for people to make the decision to give or rededicate their lives to Jesus. Generally there is also an opportunity for personal prayer, some additional resources, and connecting with other believers. So the goal of your funnel is to get people to visit your church during a service or watch a livestream.

Reaching the end goal of your marketing funnel has a specific terminology, and it is a word that is probably familiar to you. In marketing, once your funnel has successfully taken someone from the top, all the way through the funnel, it is called a "conversion." As Christians, we use the term "conversion" when referencing someone making a decision for Jesus, but for the purposes of this book, we will use the term "conversion" in reference to someone completing your funnel. Therefore, the conversion in your church marketing funnel is when someone steps foot onto your church grounds for the first time or fills out a Plan Your Visit form.

Now that you have a basic understanding of the concept of the marketing funnel, we can take a deeper look at what that looks like for your church's marketing.

Let's dive into the funnel.

THE TOP OF THE FUNNEL: THE RELATIONSHIP.

WHAT'S THE DIFFERENCE BETWEEN A NORMAL AD, AND A TOP OF THE FUNNEL AD?

The top of the funnel is your chance to make a first impression—where people connect with you for the first time, and you have the chance to introduce what your church is all about. This is where most churches screw it up. All the time I see top of the funnel church ads asking people to come visit a service, invite a friend, or attend an upcoming event. Please stop doing that.

People first need to know you and like you, and even trust you before you ask them to take a next step.

You have to build rapport with people. Only then will they be interested in taking any next steps with you. If you ask your top of the funnel audience to come visit your church, it's like asking someone to go from A all the way to Z, and skipping everything in between.

Simply put, your top of the funnel audience is defined as a list of people who don't already attend your church. Outside of the people who already attend a different church, these are the people whom you are trying to reach. **With these people, you have one very specific job, and one job only.**

Are you ready for it? **Start a positive relationship.** If you try to get anything else out of the top of the funnel, you have missed the whole point.

When you fully understand the funnel, then you will have success with your marketing efforts to the people you want to reach. However, without understanding the funnel, you will see very limited results, and you may actually do damage to your church's reputation. **Did you read that?** You may actually hurt your cause if you don't respect the process of the funnel.

If people's first impression of you is that you want something from them, they are going to have sales resistance. **This is the ultimate fail.** Once people have sales resistance, they are almost impossible to win back. Now you may be wondering, what exactly is sales resistance? Consider the feeling you get when walking into a car dealership or a furniture store. As soon as you walk through the door, you are bombarded with sales people trying to convince you to buy something. They are not there to help you really, and everybody knows that. They are only there to sell. And so you become guarded and on the defense. This is sales resistance. When you have sales resistance, you want to leave as quickly as possible. At least that is my experience.

Recently my wife Sarah and I, with our two young kids, visited a furniture store in downtown San Luis Obispo, near where we live. We were looking around for a new sectional sofa for our living room. We had been looking at a few of the big box stores, but I had been wanting to try this new local store for a while, so we stopped in to look at their selections. I couldn't even enjoy my experience and browse around, because as soon as we walked through the door, there was a salesperson waiting for us. He had a clipboard in hand, a huge smile, and the classic dress shirt tucked into blue jeans. Note to self: never trust anyone who tucks their dress shirt into jeans! (I digress). This guy simply would not let us just browse. He followed us everywhere and asked us all of his rehearsed questions. Sarah is so kind that she engaged with him the whole time, but I just really wanted to look around in peace. I know this guy was only doing his job. I also know that this tactic probably does close a lot of sales. My distaste is nothing personal towards him, but I am telling you, I will never go back to that store. I wanted to first feel comfortable and look around on my own before being forced into a sales pitch, so we left after only a short stay in the store and ended up buying a sofa online where we could browse at our leisure.

So my message to churches is this: don't be a sofa salesman. Churches can have the same negative impact as this poor sales guy in the furniture store. You don't want people to see a post from your church in their social media feed that constantly asks them to consider donating or attending or joining. Let people get to know you first. The invite can come later.

You cannot have a hidden motive. People know when something is genuine, and when it is not. **Don't publish content or ads in the top of your funnel only because you want people to come to your church. You must not do this.** You have to pour genuine love into the top of the funnel without expecting anything in return—solely because you want to impact the people you are reaching. Don't even have a hint of a hidden agenda. If they want to take the next step with your church, then great! If not, love them from a distance through online media. Sometimes that's as good as it's gonna get. When your motive is pure, only then will it produce the results you've been longing for.

Win trust with your community first. Then ask for something later. Win trust by being trustworthy. Let everything you publish to the top of your funnel be truly helpful and genuine. The top of your funnel has one purpose: to build relationships by adding value to the people in your community, and asking for nothing in return. **Add as much value as you possibly can with the time and resources at your disposal.** You need to intentionally build your reputation and the feeling people have about your church. Why? So you can lead them deeper later.

In the corporate world, this is a part of the branding process. If done correctly, you can actually shape the feeling and perception people have of your brand. It establishes your reputation as a place that genuinely cares, and you are going to get way more people to trust you with the next step in their faith journey because you have shown them that you are trustworthy. Even further than getting people to trust you, they have to like you. Give them weeks, months, years, and decades of love and value. However long it takes. The funnel never stops, so when they are ready to go deeper, you are ready to receive them. You should give so much to the top of your funnel that it hurts. Give your best.

It is hard to find consistent ways to resource and encourage people through media channels. It takes creativity, time, energy, and money. You should be spending most of your advertising money on your top of the funnel campaigns. **But don't give up, because this is where the battle is won.** You will make a deep impact when you constantly give your community something of true value, something that can positively impact their lives. And if they never come to your church because of it, that's ok. **Let that be your heart.**

Here are some great examples of top of the funnel campaigns that churches have done:

1. Write a blog post that gives helpful insights on how to improve your marriage, and post it on Facebook to encourage and strengthen local families.

2. Do a surprise meal for your local first responders to say thank you for their service, record a video surprising them with it, and post a tribute online.

3. Publish a one-minute clip of the key points of a recent message on hope, and tell people on Instagram that whatever they are going through, there is still hope.

4. Go to local farmers' markets or community events and pass out free bottled water and encourage people.

5. Promote a Facebook post inviting anyone to anonymously submit prayer requests for your staff to personally pray for.

6. Do a well-done post highlighting a local business, just to support them. Write a short article about the history of the business and introduce readers to the owner.

Those are some ideas, but there are certainly more things to do than this list. Put your creative abilities to work and continue to find unique ways to add value to your community. **Do one new top of the funnel promotion every single week.** This can be from an Instagram ad, a Facebook post, a Google ad, or even a mailer. This will simply be something that causes the community to know about you and receive some sort of message from you. The top of your funnel is where you cast a wide net to as many people as you can who are in your target area. Some of your promotions will have a huge impact, and some won't really catch on. But never stop. Give as much as you can. Create as much deeply impactful content as you can. Genuinely help people. **If you put tremendous effort into the top of your funnel, you will have tremendous results.** Remember, your ministry isn't only on Sundays anymore.

Some of the fruits of your funnel won't be known until you walk into Heaven and meet the people whom you impacted but you never even met.

Read that last sentence again.

When you are first beginning this process, be careful to manage your expectations. In the top of the funnel phase, you won't produce massive results during the first few impressions. Have patience.

You may be familiar with the idea of making an impression, but when speaking of marketing, the term impression takes on a whole new meaning. An "impression" is simply the term for when someone sees an ad or post. People usually need to see an ad quite a few times before they stop and really read or engage with it. Generally it takes about seven impressions before a person will take action on an ad. It's going to take time before you start seeing real conversions of people who make it all the way through the funnel. If your church is faithful in creating one piece of top of the funnel content every week, it is a good rule of thumb to assume that it will take around seven weeks before you start to see conversions. Pace yourself, have endurance, and be committed to investing into your top of the funnel…forever. Every week, no matter what. Galatians 6:9 says, "Let us not become weary in doing good, for at the proper time we will reap a harvest if we do not give up." So pour into people, and then do it again. I promise, you will impact them for the Kingdom.

The top of your funnel should be your best content, not your leftovers.

Also keep in mind that when I talk about an "ad," it simply means it is a piece of content that you are paying for people to see. Organic posts on social media are not ads, unless you pay to promote them. Although the word ad implies that you are trying to sell something, this is still about the top of the funnel—about reaching people and pouring into the community. It's simply the term we use, so don't get weirded out. We are paying for people to see the top of the funnel content, thus it is an ad. That doesn't necessarily mean that we are selling something.

The top of the funnel is not just a social media thing. You can be creative and find ways to impact people anywhere. You don't want to put all of your eggs into the basket of social media ads, or the basket of Google Ads. You want to get as many people from your target audience as physically possible to see your top of the funnel content on a weekly basis. You need constant ads on Facebook, Instagram, Google, and YouTube. You may even sometimes send out mailers, or have a billboard ad, or anything else that is relevant. **The more people you can get in the top of your funnel, the more conversions you will see at the bottom of your funnel.** As I write this book in 2020, the best way to reach the top of the funnel people is on Instagram and Facebook. But whatever outlets your target audience gives their time and attention to, that is what you should be investing your time and content in.

Once someone sees your content, and decides to take the next step in interacting with your church online in any way, this automatically moves them into phase two of your funnel. This is where we go for "the ask."

Welcome to the middle of the funnel.

THE MIDDLE OF THE FUNNEL: THE ASK.

SO HOW DO I MAKE THIS WHOLE RETARGETING THING WORK?

Now that you have put in the effort, and you've gotten the top of your funnel set up and working, take a moment to celebrate! People are starting to know what your church is all about, and they are beginning to trust you. Now it's time to invite them to take the next step. We don't ask for anything in the top of the funnel, but in phase two, "the ask," you request for them to come and check out your church online or in person. This is your chance to convert them from knowing who you are, to receiving from you on a spiritual level.

Here is how it works: you have a separate set of posts or videos that **you only show to people who have first engaged with one of your top of the funnel ads.**

How do you show ads to only those specific people?

This is a process called "retargeting" and is the top secret ingredient in the funnel. In the marketing industry, retargeting is a term for showing different ads to people who visit your website for the first time or engage with a post on social media. For example, if you go online to a major retailer's website right now, I can almost guarantee that the next time you open Facebook or Instagram you will now see retargeting ads from that company. Why do they do this? Because it is a much smarter use of advertising money if you spend it on people who are interested, instead of showing ads to everybody. Imagine a world where you are able to only show ads to people who are currently interested in checking out your church, instead of wasting it on people who are not interested at all. You would be more than willing to spend that money, because you know it is going to produce results.

This is exactly why companies do anything they can to figure out who is interested in their products, then show their advertisements solely to that audience. With Google and Facebook, you can use tracking codes to build a custom "audience" of people who have interacted with your church online and have shown interest. You only show your middle of the funnel content to this custom audience. **This is retargeting, and this is the middle of your funnel.** In the Paid Ads chapter of this book, I will show you exactly how to set this up for your church.

Here is a cool thought. We are taking the exact same tactics and strategies used by multi-million dollar corporations, and using them to impact people's lives for eternity. It has taken the marketing world years to figure out how sales funnels impact people's decision making, and now you can use this same funnel to introduce people to Jesus. The process works, but the motive is different.

Here is a real life example from a local church leader. Let's call him Greg. Greg wrote an article that offers practical tips and biblical insights for overcoming fear and anxiety. He spent time studying and writing the article in a very encouraging and helpful way and posted it on their church's website. They also shot a short, thirty-second promo video to let people know what the article is about. Greg's prayer was that God would use this promotion to help someone who was struggling with anxiety and could use some encouragement. Greg had a budget of $15 per day and promoted the article as an ad on Facebook, Instagram, and Google to his top of the funnel audience. Over the next three weeks there were over 7,400 people who saw the ad, and 433 people clicked on the link to his article. He had twenty-three comments and five shares. Pretty good! **But it didn't stop there.**

Because of the tracking codes and custom retargeting audience set up, all 433 people who engaged with that post were immediately added to Greg's retargeting audience. So now they are starting to see a personal invitation from Greg on their Instagram feed inviting them to check out the current series on fear and anxiety at their church. In his retargeting ad, Greg talks about how this series goes deep into this topic, and he invites people to watch their livestream or visit them in person. Every one of those 433 people have gone from the top of the funnel to the middle of the funnel. This happens automatically with Facebook's and Google Ads' custom audiences. Your job is simply to produce the message, and people get taken on the journey without any further prompting. Over the three weeks of promoting this article, Greg saw twelve new people fill out a Plan Your Visit form from this funnel.

These twelve people went from the top of the funnel, into the middle of the funnel, and then converted through the bottom of the funnel.

This is how the funnel works, and it changes people's lives.

You should be running a new top of the funnel ad every week. In addition, you should be updating your middle of the funnel (retargeting) ads once every two or three weeks. Someone in the middle of the funnel will see your retargeting content on high rotation in their social media feed, meaning that they will probably see the retargeting ads two to four times per week. That's a lot. This is why it is so important to make sure you are updating your retargeting ads on a regular basis. You should have around three to five retargeting ads all running at the same time. This way people will see a healthy rotation of ads, instead of the same one over and over. The retargeting ads don't have to be super specific like Greg's was, it can just be a general invitation to come visit your church on a Sunday. However, it can be very specific if you want. It just depends on how much time you can dedicate to it.

One of my favorite churches in Los Angeles uses the funnel to help boost attendance to their annual conferences. For the top of the funnel they use clips from the keynote speakers, and then a follow-up retargeting ad is shown with the details of the conference and a link to buy tickets. The process is still the same—they start by offering a helpful post from the keynote speaker filled with good and encouraging content, and the conference invite does not come until the middle of the funnel. People's first impression is a video that gets them excited about the keynote speakers, and then they are primed to be shown the retargeting ad to buy the tickets.

Similarly, a great church that we work with in Florida does a sixty-second clip each week recapping the message from Sunday. They promote the video as a top of the funnel ad on both Facebook and Instagram. Everyone who watches the clip will then start seeing personal invitations from the lead pastor to an upcoming Sunday. The message recap is the top of the funnel, and the personal invite by the pastor is the middle of the funnel.

Are you seeing a pattern?

In order to make the middle of the funnel effective, you have to make sure the call to action is clear and easy. Many churches use the Plan Your Visit model to give users a well-defined next step. This works great for some people, but by far, most first-time guests will just show up on Sunday and not even use the Plan Your Visit option. But even if they don't go through with filling out the Plan Your Visit form, the content on that "Visit Us" page on your website will still be very helpful in converting them to a visitor. Some churches encourage people to join them online for their livestream as the call to action, which can be very effective as well. **You can start impacting people online, before they even make it through your doors for the first time.**

The key is to be consistent and relentless. It is totally common that people will go from the top of the funnel, to the middle of the funnel and never go any further. This is absolutely normal and to be expected. You want to show those retargeting ads for around sixty to ninety days. We have found that anything longer than ninety days loses its effectiveness. If people don't respond within that sixty to ninety day window, that is ok. They go back to the top of the funnel. The next time they interact with one of the top of the funnel posts, it starts the whole process over again. Just keep it going!

The beautiful part about the middle of the funnel is that it costs less than the top of the funnel. Generally a church has a top of the funnel target audience around 300,000 people, depending on the location. But since the middle of the funnel ads are only shown to select people in the retargeting audience, you generally have only around 2,000 to 6,000 people in that audience, way less than the top of the funnel. This means that you don't have to spend nearly as much ad budget to reach those people. Fewer impressions costs less money. We will discuss budgets in a later chapter and dive into the practical details of setting up your ads and campaigns.

Now that you understand the top and the middle of the funnel, let's talk about the bottom of the funnel.

Bottoms up!

THE BOTTOM OF THE FUNNEL: THE CONVERSION.

YOUR TARGET AUDIENCE MADE IT THROUGH THE FUNNEL! NOW WHAT?

Congratulations, your funnel worked! People saw your top of the funnel ads, and they liked what they saw. Next they saw your middle of the funnel retargeting ads, and they have decided to take the next step. They are ready to respond!

The first thing we need to discuss is your conversion model. Will everyone who converts from your funnel actually show up? No. There will likely be a huge discrepancy between the people who respond, and those who actually show up. This is discouraging when you run an ad for a specific event that five hundred people sign up for, but then only one hundred people attend. One way to help prevent this discrepancy is to have a strong conversion set up. You must have some sort of a hook—something that makes people really excited to attend. If you don't have a solid conversion model in place, all the work and resources that you put into the top and middle of your funnel will be for nothing.

One option is to have a time-sensitive offer. A carrot at the end of the stick that compels people to follow through with their decision. For a first-time Sunday visitor, a great way to do this is to offer a welcome gift as part of the conversion. People can claim their gift basket online by filling out a special contact form. For example, you could have a retargeting ad send them to a Plan Your Visit form that they are then asked to fill out. We will discuss the Plan Your Visit page and how to make it perfect later when we discuss websites. But to give a brief definition, the Plan Your Visit page is where someone can fill out a form online that allows them to essentially pre-schedule their upcoming visit. After they fill out the Plan Your Visit form, you then tell them to come on Sunday and they will have a personalized gift basket waiting for them. It will include a hoodie or a shirt, a mug, a book, and maybe even a $10 gift card to go grab lunch afterwards. It doesn't have to be this gift basket specifically, but whatever you do, get creative with it and put forth the time and effort to make it a worthwhile gift. In this gift basket example, you would let them take the time to select their hoodie size, and give them a couple of options for their gift card. The point is to let them customize their first-time gift basket. This lets them know that someone is physically putting the basket together specifically for them. There is a strategy here. Knowing that someone went through all that work to set up their gift basket, people might feel bad backing out on their plans to visit. To help reel in the possible no-shows, you can make it so that the gift basket is good for that one specific Sunday only, unless they let the church know in advance that they have to reschedule their visit. Believe it or not, these things really help to firm up their decision to actually follow through and attend on Sunday.

Once you have officially decided on your conversion offer, you need to **perfect the art of follow up.** Many churches are taking advantage of automated text messaging to help remind people of their upcoming visit. Text messages are the king of follow up because they are very personal and there are so many ways to utilize them. You can have an automated text message confirming your visitor's selections for their customized gift basket. Then you can have an automated text message sent to them on Saturday reminding them of service times the following day. And on Sunday morning, one hour before the service, you could give them even further instructions. If you want to go even deeper beyond text messages, you could set up an automated email drip campaign that sends them a welcome from the pastor a day after they register. After their first service, you could also follow up with them and ask them to let you know how their experience was. All of these follow up automated events can be set up manually by connecting your website with an API platform like Zapier, or you could use one of the many drip campaign programs available.

Keep in mind that sometimes automating is ideal, but sometimes a personal touch is better. A church that I work with in California is killing it with text message follow ups. Instead of automating everything, they decided that a personal interaction was key. As soon as someone signs up for a visitor form online, they have a team member personally shoot them a text message to introduce themselves. And on Saturday or Sunday, this individual sets a time to meet them and welcome them into the church. After the Sunday service, this team member also follows up with them to see how they liked their experience. Then the following week, they invite them to lunch after church. The goal is to get people to come back three to four weeks in a row so they can build some relationships.

If your goal is to get someone to come to your church on a Sunday, there are two unique challenges. As opposed to traditional sales, people can't immediately respond to your ads. They have to wait until the next service to attend. With online sales, once they have made up their mind to purchase something, they can do so right there on the website. It is easy to measure your cost per sale, and scale your marketing with that data. But with church marketing, the only way to get real data is by using a Plan Your Visit form with some sort of offer. It is a win for churches because they can directly see the fruits of their marketing funnel. When you get a Plan Your Visit form, Facebook or Google will show you that you got a "conversion" from your funnel, and that feels pretty good! **Measuring your cost per conversion is key.**

But even if you have the best Plan Your Visit page, a killer follow up plan, and a great first-time guest gift, you still have one more problem. Most people are not going to use the Plan Your Visit form, but they are just going to show up on Sunday. Which is still great! You will be so happy when you consistently have new people coming in on Sundays. However, you will have to keep that in mind when you think about how many new visitors you can attribute directly to your marketing. The people who just show up without using the Plan Your Visit form won't be counted into your cost per conversion. So you will just have to rely on other methods of measuring where those guests are generated from.

Make sure your visitor info card or connection card (or whatever you call it at your church) has a spot where people can let you know where they first heard about you. However, don't get caught up if visitors are not checking the "Facebook" or "Instagram" options as much as you would like. Most people will hear about your church from Facebook, then Instagram, then their friend Mike, and the list goes on. It is rare that someone just hears about a church from one single location. It is all part of the funnel.

Remember, the goal of the funnel is to keep people, not just generate first-time guests. The nature of your church should be to make people feel so incredibly welcomed when they come for the first time. People should know without a doubt that guests are a big deal. Your greeters and guest experience volunteers are way more important than you may realize, but everyone should be on a mission to be as welcoming and relational as possible for new guests. Don't let your church be consumers only. Keep in mind that a guest is a life that needs to be touched. Obviously you don't want to overwhelm them, but it is a culture of kindness that people will remember more than any message or song.

Maximize your conversions with follow up and a personalized experience.

LONG TERM RELATIONSHIPS.

conversions

+

personalized experience

+

follow up

SECRET FOUR

STRATEGIC BRANDING.

BRANDING OVERVIEW.

WE'VE GOT A LOGO, SO WE'RE GOOD. RIGHT?

Before we dive even deeper into advertising, we need to talk about your branding. Branding is a big deal. Possibly even bigger than you realize. It is the foundation of your marketing. You need to be willing to do surgery on your brand. You must to be willing to rip it apart, then piece it back together, reforming it into something better. Then do it again. And again. And keep doing it until it is perfect. **Your brand needs to be intentional, strategic, and fully understood.** It's so much more than just a logo.

As you read this chapter, please know that the word "brand" and "logo" are not the same thing. Your logo is a part of your branding, but it is not an all-inclusive definition of your brand. **Your brand, simply put, is your vibe.** The feeling that one has when they experience your church, is your brand. That feeling is created by your logo, colors, font type, music, interior design, the clothing you wear, the voice in your social media posts… these are all an intentional creation of your vibe. This is either created with intentionality, or it is formed by default.

I have had the opportunity to help countless churches through the process of creating their marketing and branding. How much thought have you put into your brand? In a worst-case scenario, you have a logo that you have stuck with, simply because it seems fine. A best-case scenario is when you have fully established a brand guidelines and best practices booklet, and have intentionally chosen your voice, style guides, and colors. You need to realize that your branding is so much deeper than your logo—every media output from your church is establishing your brand.

Believe it or not, your church's branding affects people's feelings about your church. People have a certain set of emotions when they interact with your brand, and they are rarely even aware of it. What do people feel when they hear your church's name? **Branding is sub-conscious, subtle, and sneaky.** It is so much more of a feeling thing than a science thing, and that's why it is one of the most dangerous parts of marketing. You forget about your branding. You get used to your branding. And once it is set, it is difficult to change. I encourage you to read this chapter with an open mind, and be willing to make the difficult changes if they are needed.

Your branding can either be an asset or a liability. There is no middle ground.

THE GOAL OF YOUR BRAND.

OUR BRANDING IS SUPPOSED TO TELL OUR STORY, RIGHT?

This scenario has played out hundreds of times with our team: we will be on a video consultation with a church about the rebranding process, and they start talking about their backstory and how they started the church and how they are really into the contemporary look…or rustic…or whatever. It's almost always the same. I don't stop them, because I want to fully understand them and their style preferences. However, about halfway through the process they start to realize that the questions we are asking them are different than they expected.

Instead of asking the leadership team about their backstory, their favorite colors, and their design preferences, we have a totally different set of questions. **We start asking about the people in their target audience.** We ask about the city, the culture, and the neighborhood. We want to know about the most popular restaurants in their area. We want to know what people do for fun in their area. We ask them to paint a picture of their specific target demographic, what they are like, what they wear, what music they listen to. Anything and everything we can find out about their target audience, that's what we want to know. We are less interested in telling the story of their church—we want the branding to connect with their community.

The biggest and most successful brands don't have logos and colors that are focused inwardly. The best brands are created intentionally and specifically to evoke a desired feeling from their audience.

Have you noticed how pretty much all fast food restaurants use the same shade of red in their branding? Or how almost all charities and nonprofits use a similar shade of blue somewhere in their branding? Notice also how many luxury clothing and jewelry brands use serif fonts, like Rolex, Vogue, Dior, and Louis Vuitton. These brands are being strategic to evoke an emotion with their audience. Multi-million dollar corporations obsess over every element of their branding. McDonald's wants you to feel hungry. Charities want to evoke a sense of purity and goodness. The owners of Rolex want you to associate a luxurious feeling with their watches. The list goes on.

We have already solidified the fact that you should be very specific about who your target audience is. I would go even further to say that you should design your entire brand to attract one target individual. Wait, what? Yes, design your whole strategy as if it were geared to attract one specific person. You must be incredibly specific. You should build a pretend person who fits that exact target demographic, and imagine your entire brand to be built to attract this one, single person. For example, you could decide that your person is a 29-year-old male, who likes to eat at (insert your local restaurants), who likes outdoor sports like hiking, camping and fishing, and who works in sales. Obviously you would prayerfully put together your specific person that you sense God is leading you to reach. The more detailed you get, the better.

Once you have painted the picture of this target person,

you can add elements into your branding that would attract him or her. It may feel like you are being too specific, and that your church will not be attractive to the masses. But you will just have to trust me on this, being specific to one target does not subtract, it adds. In the same way that the store Whole Foods is built for a specific type of person, but is vastly popular amongst a wide range of individuals, so it will be for your church's branding. Although you have one specific person type in mind, there will be thousands of people who perfectly resonate with your branding. To reach more, focus on fewer.

One of the practical tools we use when creating branding is called a mood board. After we define a target demographic, we then put together a collage of images, fonts, words, abstract graphic elements, color bars, and unique shapes. See the example below.

The goal of a mood board is to use a wide range of artistic elements to create a feeling, or vibe, that would holistically be appealing to your target individual. It is all about feeling. After everyone agrees that the mood board evokes the right feeling, it is then used as the basis for all future branding and media. Would your logo perfectly fit as an additional image on that mood board, or would it clash? Would that sermon series artwork design fit in the mood board, or not? What changes could you make to your lobby and campus to better fit your mood board? The goal of your branding is to be attractive to your target audience, instead of just expressing your own story. When it is done strategically, your branding will be an outreach tool.

You might be wondering, what if our own church wouldn't even fit on our mood board? Don't we want to be authentic with our branding? The answer is yes, you definitely want your branding to be authentic. Recently I had a church tell me that they wanted to attract millennials to their church, and they wanted to make their branding incredibly modern and sleek. The mood board that they wanted felt like a young, rock and roll style church. But this look didn't match what this church was really like on Sundays. If they went with this style of branding, people would come and feel like they must be in the wrong place, because the branding did not match who the church really was.

You obviously don't want to portray an image that is not who you really are. Be aware that any advice in this chapter can be taken to an extreme and become ineffective. The purpose of this section is to change your perspective and motive when it comes to branding, but if you look at your mood board, and you feel that it is way too far from who you are, the problem may be that you have chosen the wrong target audience. **You have to be both authentic, and intentionally attractive at the same time.**

Sometimes you need to define a target audience that is closer to who you naturally are.

But always remember, your branding is not about you, it is about the people you are trying to reach.

CHOOSING YOUR COLORS.

HOW DO I KNOW WHAT COLORS TO USE IN OUR BRANDING?

More than any other parts of your branding, choosing the right colors will make the biggest impact on people's emotions. More than font type, more than the icon. It is vital that you choose your colors carefully, intentionally, and strategically.

Not long ago, we decided that we needed to redo the colors for our own company. We felt like we needed to be more intentional with communicating the right feelings to our audience, so our team sat down and discussed some possibilities regarding colors, and played with some different gradient color shades. After a lot of thought and creative meetings, we made the decision to simply stick with science. We chose a shade of orange that studies have shown communicate a sense of freshness and newness. It was already a proven color shade, so we went with it. This has turned out to be a great decision for us. We were completely pleased with the logo and how it translated onto our website and social media grid.

For your church, you could choose to read articles and research the exact way that certain color shades affect the human brain, and do your own experimenting. Or you could go with what are already the trusted rules of thumb by industry standards. Here are some well-documented findings about color schemes and the feelings they evoke:

Deep blue - trustworthiness, wisdom, and expertise
Light blue - charity, purity, and wholesomeness
Yellow - happiness, hope, and optimism
Orange - new, fresh, and young
Purple - royal, regal, and mature
Deep green - organic, wealth, and success
Black - elegance, power, and depth
Tan - earthy, natural, and warmth

While this list is a good starting place, don't use it as the sole deciding factor when choosing your color. What's most important is evoking the right feeling for your specific audience. Every age group, community, and even city has unique traits that need to be considered when choosing your colors. As an example, if your church's branding uses colors that are similar to a large local company, people will subconsciously transfer some of their feelings about that company to your brand. As silly as it sounds, you should also consider the colors of local and rival sports teams. Some people who just read that will think I am crazy for making that suggestion, but some of you will absolutely get it!

Furthermore, pay attention to other churches in your area, and make sure to avoid using very similar colors and font type to them. Almost every church has a unique individual target person, and there are plenty of colors and branding options to go around, so do some research when making your decision.

Also keep in mind that every logo should ideally have one main color, and one complimentary color. I do not recommend having more than two colors in your official logo. Your mood board will have a palette of colors for all media output, but your logo should stick with just two. However, if you want to choose just one color for your logo, that could work as well. Choosing just one bold color would pair well with black or white and often be sufficient enough by itself.

A great process for choosing your colors is to step back and take a wide view of your mood board. Intentionally or not, there will probably be some colors that really stick out in this collage of images. I suggest choosing your primary and your secondary colors directly from your mood board. Find the primary color that evokes the right emotion for your specific target audience, and use the exact color tone for your logo.

While your logo color scheme is important, the colors you choose go beyond just what is in your logo. Your mood board will usually have five to eight colors that are allowed in your non-logo branding collateral. For example, your website should use the colors of your branding in the design elements. Your interior paint colors should also fit in your branding, and even the filtering on the photos in your Instagram feed should be intentional and on-brand.

Choose wisely, because colors matter.

COLORS
MATTER.

- Charity
- Purity
- Wholesomeness

- New
- Fresh
- Young

- Trustworthiness
- Wisdom
- Expertise

- Happiness
- Hope
- Optimism

- Organic
- Wealth
- Success

- Earthy
- Natural
- Warmth

- Royal
- Regal
- Mature

- Elegance
- Power
- Depth

TIMELESS BRANDING.

HOW CAN OUR BRANDING STAND THE TEST OF TIME?

As you read this book, there are current popular graphic design trends for font, effects, styles, and colors, but something to keep in mind: styles change over time. Blink twice and today's trends will look dated and old. I can guarantee you that design styles have changed even since the day this chapter was written. A big mistake that you can make with your branding is to be too tied to today's current trends. However, this poses a unique challenge. How can you be relevant to today's culture without risking being dated tomorrow?

In the church world, design trends last for about two to three years. After that, they start to look worn out, like LeBron James' hairline (if you know, you know). Many churches want to be relevant and contemporary with their brand image, and depending on your target audience, that can be a very smart goal. Be careful, though, or you might use too many trendy style elements that are only going to be relevant for a few years. **Once your branding looks dated, you won't be able to make minor tweaks and brand updates. You will have to start over.** Sometimes that is ok. Starting over is a great way to refocus your goals and target audiences, but it can also be very expensive and difficult.

The best way to prevent your branding from having a short shelf life is to make your logo simple. A simple logo is almost timeless. In our agency, when we go through the logo design process with churches, we start with three or four concepts that evoke the right emotions. Getting the feeling right is our top priority, so while these first concepts might not be polished enough to be an official logo, we give them consideration because the emotions are right. Furthermore, most of the beginning versions will only have words, and no icon. What we have found is that having the right font type and style is most important, so we focus on this first. After we choose the font and layout, then we add icons. After trying out a few more versions, we then eliminate and cut out as much as we can from the logo we like best. We simplify it as much as possible, without diminishing the design. When we do this, we can usually find many little details that were not adding any value and were just cluttering up the design. The end result is a logo that is clean, simple, and as timeless as we can get.

Simplicity in church branding is rare to find. Especially when dealing with icons. For churches, the least number of doves flying out of steeples and spreading their wings over crosses, the better. And the sooner your church understands this, the better.

If you have successfully designed a logo that will endure the test of time, **you will still have to update your branding, just less frequently.** When branding is done well from the inception, it will not need a rebrand. But it will need something called a brand refresh. A rebrand is when you start completely over. A brand refresh is when you take your current logo, and make subtle tweaks and adjustments to give it a more contemporary look. It's like a facelift for your branding. A good example of this is when Southwest Airlines changed their icon from an airplane above the word "Southwest" to the new logo that says "Southwest" with a heart as the period. Another example is the restaurant chain Olive Garden, who previously had a photo-realistic style logo, which they changed to a graphical logo. These were not new branding creations, they were subtle modifications to adjust to current design standards.

Your church will also need to make these small changes to stay current, but this job is much less stressful when the original design is simple and easy to manipulate.

Be simple. Be timeless.

FOCUS ON HOW YOU TALK.

DOES THE WAY WE TALK AND WRITE AFFECT OUR BRANDING?

Remember, your branding is all about your vibe. It is the feeling that your brand evokes, but this feeling is not just created with colors, font type, and designs. It is also created with your voice.

When I talk about your voice, I'm talking about the language you use. Both in the written and the spoken word. Do you have a formal voice? Should you use slang and casual language? How do you use humor? These are all communication styles that help to create the way people perceive you. In order to be intentional with your branding, you should be intentional with your voicing.

Think of it this way. If there was a photo posted on Instagram by Charles Stanley's church, and an identical image posted on the Instagram account of Andy Stanley's church, their captions would probably be very different. Each of these churches has its own style and vibe. They have different target audiences, different leadership styles, and very different brands. You could almost recognize the differences in their brands simply by their voices. This is another great example of how branding is not just visual, but so many other details must be taken into account.

Your voice should be intentional. Let's look at Starbucks as an example and examine how they talk on their social media posts to create a specific vibe. With every post of a perfect latte, they use captions that are short, playful, and classy. This reinforces a brand experience with Starbucks that is both contemporary and sophisticated at the same time. An Instagram post in December shows a beautiful butterscotch latte sitting on a table that overlooks a blizzard outside. The caption simply says "Cozy as can be. #SmokedButterscotchLatte." The caption is short and casual sounding, and the image conveys a sense of warmth and comfort. All of their posts convey these same fun yet classy vibes, which is what their customers start to sense about the brand as a whole. **You need to think about your target audience, and speak in a way that is attractive to them.**

Your communication style should even be specified in your brand guidelines book, which we will talk about in the next section. As your church grows, you are going to have more and more people on your media team. If you don't specifically define your voice, then every time a social post is written, or an email blast is sent out, it will all sound different. You need to define it and communicate it to your team. Even the titles of your message series or your events should take your branding voice into consideration.

If your church is targeting an older, more established demographic, then have your voice be elegant, traditional, and gentle. If your church is targeting college aged students, then your voice should be minimal, witty, and somewhat playfully sarcastic. For a church that targets young families, use a voice that is nurturing and gentle. If you target young professionals, use a more professional voice. Every demographic and audience has unique and subtle differences in how they communicate. Learn it, speak it, and adapt to it.

Decide how you talk, and make it intentional.

Pro Tip - Follow a lot of the companies, athletes, and musicians that are popular with your target audience. Many of the ways that people communicate are taken from social media content published by influencers online. If you follow them and pay attention to their voice, you will start to naturally adapt.

OFFICIAL BRAND GUIDELINES BOOK.

DO WE REALLY NEED TO HAVE ALL OF THIS WRITTEN OUT? WON'T PEOPLE JUST CATCH OUR VIBE?

As a leader, it can be really frustrating when the people on your team can't read your mind, right? I mean, why don't they know exactly what I want them to do, all the time, and do it exactly the way I want it done? Obviously I am joking, but the truth is, sometimes we make assumptions like this without even realizing it.

The people on your marketing team want to follow the branding of the church. They want to know your voice and style. But they will be left feeling insecure and unsure without having clearly defined standards to follow. I used to think that creatives should be left to do whatever they want, but after years of overseeing graphic designers and social media marketers, I have learned that creative people appreciate specific guidelines. Their creativity actually flourishes within the boundaries of clear direction.

That being said, everyone on your media team should be given a PDF or printed book that contains your official brand guidelines. You should review this book with your team, and give them the opportunity to ask for clarification on any of it. Take the time to train them and talk them through these guidelines. Providing your team with this resource allows you to use it as the gold standard on all media content for your church.

Your official brand guidelines book should be a document that contains a complete and clear definition of your brand. Everything from your colors and your style, all the way to your voice. It is generally a ten to twenty page PDF with all of the details that a designer or content creator would need in order to create media for your church and stay on brand. The beginning of the book should start by clearly defining your target audience and your specific target individual. Explain this person in detail, and help your team understand the reason for targeting this sample person. The next section will contain your mood board, which your media team will reference for all of their designs. The following section should provide an expanded explanation of your official logo, in all of its different versions. Clearly define your primary, secondary, and icon versions of your logo, as well as the various font types and exact colors of your design. Your logo should never be used outside of the approved formats in this official brand guidelines book.

Another very important section of your brand guidelines book is a full description of your approved fonts. All publications on print and screen should follow your clearly defined style guides. You want there to be two to four font types that are used exclusively in your media. You should define the font type for all headings and subheadings. This includes details like tracking, thickness, and color. It is common for corporations to define the space between letters, and also to define the space above and below lines of text. The type of font that you use in normal paragraphs should also be specified, including spacing and thickness. Be sure to clarify when and how to use italic fonts and bold fonts. **The more detailed you can get, the better.** ←

Even after you have defined your target audience, shown your mood board, discussed font style and the detailed break-down of your logo, you still have much more to communicate in your brand guidelines book. The next section should be all about photography. You need to specify the style of photos you want to use, and you also need to clarify the specific color filters that your brand calls for. This is a bit more abstract and diffi-cult to define, but it is very important for the people on your visual media team to understand what the style is. Give exam-ples of what kinds of shots you like to use, and give examples of what you don't like. Try not to assume that people will know what you are looking for; over directing is always better than not giving enough direction.

Your church should have specific color filters that you use on your social media photos, print material, and service screens. These color filters can change seasonally, or you can keep them consistent all year round. A great example of this is the popular grocery store Sprouts. You can follow Sprouts on Instagram and see what an excellent job they do with pulling the right colors out of every photo in their social feed. If you scroll down the grid on their Instagram account, you will see that during specific seasons they focus their feed on certain col-ors. And they change the color every season. As I look at their feed now, they are focusing on the color orange. Every photo has clearly been put into Lightroom and the colors have been tweaked to pull out the orange tones. As you scroll down the feed, it is really cool to see how the colors change from season to season. It takes a lot of planning and work to be this inten-tional with color in your media, **but these little details make a great first impression.**

In addition to defining the filters used on each photo, you should also define the types of photos you use. Do you prefer abstract shots, or straight on smiling face photos? Action shots, or candid shots? Your brand guidelines book should dedicate one full page with eight to ten example photos that evoke the right feeling for your intended branding. Your team can use that as a basis to understand what kind of media to create.

The last part of your brand guidelines book should be dedicated to defining your voice. Your unique speaking style and tone. This is the most difficult to define, as it is the most ambiguous of all the branding elements. This section should start with a short description of the tone and style of your voice, and the reasoning behind it. Next you provide sample snippets of headlines and captions that most clearly capture your tone. If you could provide at least ten great examples, it will really help your media team to grasp the vibe. After that, you should provide contrasting examples of paragraphs that do not have your tone. This will allow people to fully understand the way your voice sounds, and the way it does not.

Voice, color, mood, fonts…these things don't just happen on their own. They are choices that your team will make—so be sure that you're clearly defining your vision.

People aren't mind readers. Create the guidelines they need.

Pro Tip - If you would like an example of a completed brand guidelines book for a church, I can send you one that our team at Vibrant Agency created. Just email me at ross@vibrantagency.com and either I or one of our team members will personally email you a PDF so you can see it for yourself.

SECRET FIVE

DOMINATE ON
INSTAGRAM.

INSTAGRAM OVERVIEW.

HOW DO WE CRUSH IT ON INSTAGRAM?

Since this book was written in 2020, the strategies outlined here are specific to Instagram's features as of then, but if you are reading this and the information is outdated, don't get discouraged. The absolute beauty of marketing is that it is always changing. Some view this as frustrating, but I view it as a great opportunity. As soon as an advertising strategy gets figured out by the masses, it quickly becomes oversaturated. This means that the impact of a marketing strategy that used to work doesn't work anymore. **And that is awesome.** Why? Because people get distracted, lazy, tired, or too busy to stay on the cutting edge, so people like you and me who are hungry to find new ways of reaching people can separate ourselves from the pack. **Becoming truly great at social media marketing means never giving in to complacency.** It means always being willing to try out the new features and ideas that Instagram (IG) puts out. Don't get comfortable—get creative.

Right now, churches who don't have a deep Instagram strategy are truly hurting themselves. Every day more and more people are engaging on Instagram than they are on Facebook. This does not mean that you shouldn't have a content strategy on Facebook, but it does mean that you should be focused on Instagram in a very serious way. Not too long ago my wife was telling me how she didn't like Instagram, because she didn't get it. She preferred Facebook. But eventually she set up an Instagram account and gave it a try. Again she told me that she just didn't like it—at first—but fast forward four more weeks, and she is on Instagram way more than she is on Facebook. Now we can't go anywhere without her pulling out her phone to take some photo of her coffee or our kids and posting it on her story. This is happening to so many people all over the world, so as a church going into all the world, you should go all in on Instagram. And if you are reading this book at some point in the future when there is a new platform that is taking over, go all in on that one. For example, TikTok has been blowing up, and I can see this being the next social media platform that starts to compete with Instagram.

People are in totally different mindsets while using Instagram than they are while using Facebook. Because of this, IG and Facebook should have completely different types of posts, so don't make the mistake of posting the same exact content on both platforms. Once people sense that your post is an automated post that got pushed from a different platform, your engagement will drop. Big time. When you have a post on Facebook that has a bunch of hashtags, people are going to know that you just pushed it from Instagram, and they will stop paying attention to your Facebook content. Furthermore, if you have a post on Facebook that is an Instagram-shaped image with a cute caption that totally feels like it came from IG, it will simply not feel authentic to the Facebook platform. If you are posting something for Instagram, make it perfect for Instagram and only Instagram. It is better to let Facebook wait for a post that is better suited for its platform.

Instagram is unique. Instagram is artistic. And your church's Instagram content needs to fit what people are expecting on that platform. Also, avoid the mistake of thinking short term, by only thinking post by post. You want to be planning how your entire feed looks holistically. Is your content balanced? Does it have the right flow of colors? Do you have enough videos compared to photos? Is the vibe pulling out the emotions that you intend? Instagram has given churches such a unique opportunity to intentionally create posts with the feelings and aesthetics from their branding. It is like a never-ending mood board that allows you to continuously reinforce your brand. You can literally put out content any time you want to showcase your intended style.

The content you post on Instagram will help tell the story of who your church is. But let's be clear, the posts themselves aren't what attracts a new person in the first place. You won't reach new people just by posting on Instagram, even if they are really great posts. Yes, you read that correctly. **Go ahead and post a hundred times per day, but it is not going to make people come to your church.** Your Instagram posts are going to be seen mostly by the people who already follow you on Instagram. It seems obvious, right? But people are constantly acting like I dropped a truth bomb on them when I remind them of this. I don't care how many hashtags you use, they are not going to attract many new people. I don't care how many stories you do, they won't make an impact on people who don't follow your account. Later in this book we are going to discuss exactly how to use Instagram and Facebook to reach new people, but spoiler alert: it isn't all about what kind of content you post. The main purpose of your IG content is to reinforce your vibe. It is building your branding. If you do it right, Instagram can be a foundational pillar in building the culture of your church.

So how does your Instagram content help with marketing? If someone sees an advertisement from your funnel and they want to check you out, what is their most likely next step? They are going to view your profile. Only then will they see all of your creative and unique posts and get a sense of what you are about. That's why it's important to understand that your posts are still part of the funnel. The posts themselves don't attract a person to the top of your funnel, but when someone enters your funnel, you want to make sure your posts fit in with the style and voice from ads they have seen. Use your Instagram content to speak to that one individual whom you are targeting. Show him/her how your church is the perfect fit.

And guess what? Almost everyone under the age of forty who visits your church for the first time will have had one of their first impressions of your church be from your IG content, either from an ad or a post. Not your parking lot, not that great smiling greeter that welcomed them, not even your website. **Since your Instagram content is one of their first impressions of your church, let's make it a good one!**

Use Instagram to define your brand and make an awesome first impression.

USE YOUR SERIES FOR CONTENT.

WHAT SHOULD WE BE POSTING?

A great Instagram campaign has both high-quality content, and also a high volume of content. This can be tricky. If you are posting daily content, pretty soon you will run out of new ideas to post, then your content becomes less creative and you lose engagement. On the other hand, you might only post when it feels inspired and amazing, but waiting until inspiration strikes will create low volume, which leads to an ineffective Instagram campaign. **You must have both quality and volume,** and the only way to have both is to preschedule your posts.

If you are part of a church that utilizes themed message series, this is really helpful for your Instagram content. Often with message series, each weekend has its own key points and focus topics. Since these will likely be planned out in advance, you've got built-in content to post about. Post message reminders and recaps on the Monday, Tuesday, and Wednesday after Sunday services. This will help people remember the key takeaways and apply them to their lives, and it also gives you fresh and relevant content to post about. Keeping in theme with the design style of your current message series gives you built-in creative inspiration. This also adds depth to your posts because they are relevant to what is currently happening at the church.

A great way to keep people engaged with your messages is a sermon highlight video—a short video from your most recent message with subtitles or captions. The engagements and views generated by these videos are truly impressive. Even the most creative posts you put on Instagram will not get as much engagement as these weekly caption videos. They take some time, but they are totally worth it.

The process is like this: you take the video from the Sunday message and find some of the key moments or points. Instagram currently limits the length of videos to one minute, unless you post it as an IGTV post. This will very likely change by the time you are reading this book. Once you have trimmed the video clips to a compilation of one minute or less, it's time to add some subtitles. There is a very affordable online program called Headliner that will help generate captions for you, otherwise you will have to manually type them in. Always check for typos, because it isn't a perfect system. We use Adobe Premiere for adding style and effects to the text. It has a bit of a learning curve, but it really is not that difficult to use. Next, add some background music to the video that captures the vibe of the message, and make sure to add your website, logo, or some call to action at the end of the clip. Instagram posts are square sized, so a video size of 1080 x 1080 pixels is ideal for posts. To make the videos for Instagram stories fit perfectly on a phone screen, make the video 1080 x 1920 pixels. You can set your video output size in the settings in Premiere. I suggest doing your caption video as an IG story in addition to a post. This way it will get double the engagement. Although Instagram stories limit you to a fifteen-second clip, you can use a multitude of free apps to make your video split into fifteen-second segments so it plays almost like it is one normal-length clip.

Once you have the subtitles, correct sizing, and background music added, there are a couple more things that will really make your video great. You want to clean up the audio so people can understand the message. There are some built-in audio effects in Premiere that can really help make the words easy to understand. Adding a compressor to the audio of the message will help make the volume more consistent. Another suggestion is to add an equalizer (EQ) to the vocal track. Adobe Premiere has a built-in template that is called "Optimize for Internet Delivery" which really helps the vocals come through clearly. However, every speaking voice is different, so find out what works best for your church, and stick with it.

Once you have the audio dialed in, you have one last step. You don't want each week's message recap video to be the same styling over and over. If you can find creative ways to add design elements of the current message series into the background, colors, music, or effects of the video, that will really go a long way. Make these videos as unique as possible each week to keep your audience engaged.

Another great tip is to utilize the highlights feature on Instagram. You can save a set of IG stories that have content based on a specific sermon series. As an example, you can have clips from the messages, your caption videos, some key-point graphics, and photos, all based around a specific series. When you save these as featured highlights, people can look back years later and remember all the important points of that message series. It is really cool to see them accumulate over the months and years.

Let your message series be the foundation of your weekly content schedule, but keep it fresh and creative. **Never let your Instagram content become predictable.**

BALANCING YOUR CONTENT.

WHAT ARE THE BEST IMAGES TO USE ON INSTAGRAM?

There are two big questions that people ask me about their Instagram content. Are we posting the right images? And how often should we be posting? Let's start with the question about how often. There isn't a simple answer to this question, because each Instagram account and audience is unique. You need to pay attention to how your people respond. However, a good rule of thumb is to post high-quality content on your Instagram feed every other day. I have found this to be the sweet spot for maximum engagement for both your Instagram feed posts and your story posts. An IG story post only lasts for twenty-four hours (unless they have changed by the time you are reading this book), but every other day is still a good frequency for posting them. This means that **you should do both a high-quality Instagram feed post, and a separate Instagram story post every other day.** Yes, this is double the work, but right now, Instagram stories are getting sometimes as much as five times more engagement than traditional posts do. Therefore it is highly important to put an equal amount of effort into your Instagram stories as you do your traditional posts.

The other big question I get is about images, so let's talk about the type of media you are posting. You must find a balance with the types of content you post on Instagram—videos, photos, infographics, etc. The last thing you want to do with your Instagram grid is have a bunch of the exact same content. That's boring. I have seen churches that have 90% of their entire Instagram grid be only infographics, or text on top of background photos. Don't do that.

When someone in the top of the funnel sees an Instagram ad from your church, and they want to know more, the first thing they will do is view your Instagram profile. Not your website, not your latest message—your Instagram profile. This is why the collective view of your grid matters. You only have seconds to make a positive first impression and communicate who your church is. Make sure that you are switching up the type of content that you are posting. Find balance. Some posts should be still images with smiling faces. Some posts should be video clips. Some posts should be abstract images with creative captions, and some posts should be graphics. It is important to make sure that someone checking out your church sees a variety of different content types, which makes it feel real and organic. Never appear as predictable or robotic.

While your feed needs variety, the type of content that gets the best engagement is pictures of smiling faces. The majority of your Instagram grid should be posts of people smiling, hugging, worshiping, or anything like that. Not only does it help to set a joyful impression of your church, but it also makes your content much more noticeable and effective. **Over 50% of your grid should be filled with smiling face photos at all times.**

Beyond making sure that you balance out the visual content, it is also important to have balance with the captions on your posts. Yes your Instagram should promote and announce upcoming events, but you don't want your profile to seem like a running bulletin board. Keep internally-focused announcements to a minimum. It is also good to do quotes and captions from the most recent message, but too much deep spiritual content will make you unrelatable to outsiders. Here is a sample weekly Instagram content schedule that we use for many churches. Although we don't suggest posting seven days per week, this outline can give you an idea of what content works best on various days of the week:

Sunday: Service reminder two hours before service with message series visual.

Sunday: IG stories throughout the service, including worship and message.

Monday: Creative way to share photos from Sunday's gatherings. Story or post.

Tuesday: Short caption video from Sunday's message. Story and post.

Wednesday: Day off. Internal announcement post if needed.

Thursday: Engagement or community-focused post.

Friday: Creative sequence of stories about current sermon series.

Saturday: Reminder/teaser for Sunday service. Post and story.

Many churches use content scheduling software to help pre-schedule their posts throughout the week. This is highly recommended, because sometimes life happens, and you simply don't have time to get the right content out. Sit down once per week for a few hours and batch create most of your weekly content. It will help! There are many options out there, and we have had the opportunity to test pretty much all of them. As of the writing of this book, the best one to use is Hootsuite. However, all of the social media content schedulers are limited by Instagram's rules and regulations for third party integration, so there is no perfect solution. The main problem with using Hootsuite or any other content scheduler is that it does not have a 100% success rate. With software updates and occasional glitches, you can't have true confidence that your posts will go live when you need them to. However, it is reliable enough that it is definitely worth using. One thing that is currently unavailable is true Instagram story prescheduling, which would be very helpful. But for now, prescheduling your grid posts using Hootsuite will make your life much easier. Using a program like Hootsuite also allows for team collaboration, so you can have multiple people on your team contribute to your Instagram content schedule.

Just remember, keep it balanced, and don't be boring.

MAXIMIZING SOCIAL STORIES.

WHAT ARE THE BEST WAYS TO USE INSTAGRAM STORIES?

Let me start with the basics. Instagram stories are content that live on your profile for only twenty-four hours, unless you save them as a featured highlight story. The strategy and content for stories is completely different than for your grid. Instagram stories are for the rougher, less produced content that doesn't live forever on your beautiful Instagram grid. Stories are much more related to what is happening that specific day. You can think of Instagram stories like you would a daily journal, where you jot down the fun, mundane, or routine parts of your day. This contrasts with your Instagram grid which acts more like your family photo album. The Instagram grid is made up of the pictures that should live on forever in your photo album of life, and your Instagram stories are just the highlights and content specific to that day.

Because Instagram stories are totally different from Instagram grid posts, the strategy in producing them needs to be different as well. As of today, the content you post on your church's Instagram story will get more views than your traditional posts. Wait, say that again? Yes, your Instagram stories will get more views and responses than even your best posts. The concept of posting a traditional image and writing your caption is great, but people are most drawn to content that feels natural, raw, and fresh. When you view an Instagram story, you almost feel like you might get a glimpse of a candid moment, or a behind-the-scenes view that you wouldn't normally get with a traditional post. With this understanding of the reason why people are drawn to stories as compared to posts, this poses a unique opportunity to give people what they want to see. Let them see the raw and real you.

A good start for Instagram stories is to document everything that happens during your Sunday service. Short video clips of people in worship practice, setting up the lobby, or walking through the doors, or even snippets of the message or candid worship moments—these are all great types of content to share on your Instagram story. You should give a volunteer or team member the responsibility of documenting the entire Sunday experience specifically on Instagram stories each weekend. Yes, you need to specifically choose someone on your team to capture the Sunday experience for your stories. If you don't give someone that job, it simply won't happen.

You can (and should) buy camera equipment that is designed to enhance your phone's built-in camera. For less than $50 on Amazon, you can buy a handheld stabilizer with a clip-on shotgun mic that is built for a phone. This allows for you to shoot footage with smooth motion, and it allows for clearer audio. For less than $20, you can buy a clamp that will hold your phone on a mic stand so you can set it up to record media over an extended period of time or go hands free and interview someone. Experiment with the various add-on lenses and third-party video editing apps. It will really help take your social media story production to a new level. The key is to have one person, or a few people, take true responsibility for the Instagram story content each Sunday. If you make it a priority, then your team will start to understand how serious you are about reaching people through social media.

Crushing it on Sundays with your IG stories is a great start, but it is just that, a starting point. To do a truly excellent job on IG stories is to have creative content happening throughout the week. This takes on a whole new set of challenges. You don't have a daily worship service to document, so you have to come up with the content ideas on your own. However, not all Instagram stories need to be video content, but instead, you can use your graphics team to create designs specifically made for Instagram stories. Or even better, you can use photography. Keep in mind that the ideal image size for Instagram stories is 1080 x 1920. Please don't be the one who posts square images in IG stories.

The challenge comes in when you don't know what to post about. What if there is nothing noteworthy happening that day? This is the problem that everyone runs into, but this problem is easily overcome with a little bit of planning. Professional Instagram influencers, whose Instagram content is literally their entire livelihood, have a strategy for this exact situation. When they post a photo or a story on their account, it is rarely content that they created right on the spot. Or even that day. Or heck, even that month! When us common folk post a new Instagram story, we usually take the picture or video right there on the spot and then post it. Professionals do it quite differently. Instagram professionals have a huge bank of photos and graphics in various folders on their phone's photo app. They have loads of content in their back pockets from events that happened in the past, ready to post at any time. So when it comes time to post a new Instagram story, they aren't limited to where they are at that very moment. Instead they pull from their pre-created content folders.

A friend of mine at our office is an Instagram influencer, and I started to see this pattern whenever we were together. We would have a normal and somewhat boring day at the office, but later they would post a photo of them on a vacation, or at the beach. And the caption would say something like "thinking of Maui today" or something that references the photo. They actually live a pretty normal life, but they keep their feed going from previous events.

What does this mean for a church? This means that you can have banks of photos from your last baptism Sunday, worship night, serve day, or whatever other big events your church partakes in. Keep these events alive by using them on your stories as throwback posts. This keeps your content fresh without having to wait for the next big event. Have tons of photos and content taken each weekend of different ministries in your church. These don't all have to be shared right on Sunday, but you can plan them out through the week. Another example would be to do a shot of someone worshiping in the crowd, and do a quote of some of the lyrics from the set list that Sunday. With a little bit of planning, you could easily fill an entire week of both regular posts and Instagram stories for your church from past events.

But what about the raw and candid nature of Instagram stories? Shouldn't we be posting that kind of content throughout the week? The answer is yes, absolutely. The reason for keeping a bank of polished photos and clips for your Instagram stories is to fill the gaps when you don't have candid moments to share. Post both the candid content, and the polished content. Make it a weekly responsibility for various members of your team to film a short, thirty-second encouraging video for Instagram stories. Just holding their phones and talking, nothing produced or overly edited. Some days it can be something spiritual and from the heart, or some days it can be a shout-out about an event or ministry happening that night. Don't regulate it, but let it be organic. You have to make it a priority for there to be content up on your Instagram stories each week.

Your ministry does not happen just on Sundays anymore. Talk to people every day through stories.

PHOTOGRAPHY DONE RIGHT.

HOW DO WE GET MORE PHOTOS, AND BETTER PHOTOS, EACH WEEK?

Nobody wants to see an Instagram grid filled with stock photos. The very essence of Instagram is based on photos of experiences and of people. If you have made up your mind that Instagram is about first impressions, then make it a priority to get good photos every week.

This poses a challenge. In fact, one of the biggest struggles that we hear from churches is that they don't have enough photos to use each week on social media. You can't just wish for photos, you have to prioritize it. Make photography the Sunday responsibility for someone on the serve team. It doesn't have to be a paid staff member—someone can volunteer. You can even make an actual church ministry for the sole purpose of taking photos before, during, and after services on Sundays. In fact, I highly recommend it. If you list photography and videography as one of the ministry opportunities for a volunteer to sign up for, you will be surprised at the number of people who are interested in helping. However, keep in mind that it will be important to make a schedule if you have multiple team members, just like you would in the children's ministry. If you only have one person who is responsible for taking photos, you will run into gap weeks when that individual can't attend service for whatever reason, but if you have multiple photographers and a schedule, the volunteers can work together to cover each other when they can't make a service.

Certainly your volunteers will have varying talent levels, and that's ok. You can ask people to submit a portfolio of their photos before they volunteer, or just train them. You need training to be on the worship team, sound team, etc. Sometimes people have hidden talents that they weren't even aware of! However, if your volunteer team members simply have no creative intuition for photography, just kindly point them to a different ministry.

Make a system where you tell the media team exactly what kind of shots you are looking for each service. Give them examples of other churches who are capturing great photos every week, and have them seek to get shots with a similar feel at your church. Show them your mood board, which should include multiple photos that have the energy and vibe that your branding calls for.

All team members should share a folder in your church's Google Drive or Dropbox, and after each service they should place all of the photos they captured into that folder so the entire media team can have access to them. This is where your social media content will be pulled from each week.

But don't just stop at still photos! Your team should also capture short b-roll type clips each week. B-roll video clips are candid video clips that are raw and unscripted. Some of the best social media accounts will occasionally use a short compilation of b-roll video clips that document the whole Sunday experience. Sometimes b-roll video captures the energy of the message and worship even better than a photo can. This can be clips of worship, the message, and people in the foyer. Adding some music and text on top of this video is a relatively easy task and can get much more engagement than still images.

Sometimes you will have volunteers who already have a great camera and gear, but that shouldn't be a requirement for being on the team. Your church should have your own DSLR camera for the media team to use. You can find decent used cameras on places like Facebook Marketplace or Craigslist for under $500. If that doesn't fit in the budget, don't overlook your trusty smartphone. You will be pleasantly surprised at how incredible the photos can look on some of the newest versions of smartphones. Using some of the affordable equipment that we discussed earlier can help add the professional look to a smartphone's photos. Heck, you might even prefer it over a bulky camera!

Getting great photos in your feed is so much more than point and click, so let's talk about editing. Our philosophy is that we make a big deal about small details. Why? Because **greatness in marketing is the sum of a billion tiny details.** When pieced all together, these small details equal the overall excellence that you're needing. And one of these small details is how you edit your photos before posting them.

Your church's branding specifies a certain color guide and styling. Since every Instagram photo should fit in your mood board, that means editing the colors and tones are a must. You need to have a consistent color filtering that you do on your Instagram photos to make them fit your brand. The best way to do this is to use the Adobe program called Lightroom. In this program you can have preset filters that slightly adjust the tones and colors of each photo. If you glance through a successful company's Instagram grid, you will notice that most of the photos have a similar color tone to them, and usually that color tone will complement their overall branding. Although this is a very small detail, it will bring your professionalism to a new level. So much of branding and marketing revolves around feeling. Using specific filters will subtly evoke the right emotions as people scroll through Instagram. I know it takes extra time to add these filters. **But anything you do with marketing, you should do with excellence.**

Consistency with colors. Frequency with photos.

LOCAL WINS ON INSTAGRAM.

HOW DO WE ENGAGE WITH OUR LOCALS ON INSTAGRAM?

Most people are proud of their city. Otherwise they wouldn't live there. Therefore using Instagram to celebrate and support your local community is an excellent way to build trust with your target audience. Be strategic by focusing some of your social content outward towards your city. When you intentionally take time to post content about your local community, people will start to embrace you. You want to be a church that is not just in your community, but a part of it. **Be a church that loves your city, and your city will love you back.**

1 John 3:18 says, "Dear children, let us not love with words or speech but with actions and in truth." So don't just love your city in theory, love it with action. When there are big community events, show your pride by being there, and posting content on Instagram about it. Several options include local holiday celebrations, festivals, the opening of new businesses and restaurants, or even big high school or college sporting events. Be

there. Show your excitement and support.

One church in California is in a city that has a big weekly farmers' market. Thousands of people attend, so this church decided to get involved and rent out a booth each week. They have a big banner that says "Coffee + Jesus" behind them, and anyone who stops by the booth gets a coffee and bottled water. Totally for free, no gimmicks. They pass out church invite cards on the tables, and offer to pray for anyone who wants it. Every week they have Instagram stories and posts highlighting their farmers' market and showing how fun it is. This has really helped this church become known and loved in the community. Instead of just doing posts about it, they put their love into action by being involved.

You have to know your city and your community. There is no cookie-cutter formula with this one; it takes an actual understanding of what your city is all about. If you make this a priority for your Instagram content, your community will see how you care, and they will respond to it.

While being involved in large events is great, that's not the only way to show local support—just be a true local. A predominant church in Florida makes a big deal about small groups on their social media. They have content on their social media each week of families and friends gathering for things like dinner at a local restaurant or hanging out at the park. This allows them to celebrate that they are deeply rooted in the local culture, while at the same time promoting their small groups. **Trust me, being authentic and local is a big deal.**

Be about what your community is about. Important stuff, fun stuff, stuff that needs to change. All of it. Here is a great example of what I mean: a church that I work with is right in the heart of Alabama. Their town is pretty evenly split between their loyalties for the two rival college football teams. Half of the city is Alabama Crimson Tide fans, and the other half is Auburn Tigers fans. If you know football, then you know that the fans of those teams take it pretty seriously! One day before the first college football game of the season, we did a post on the church's Instagram that had both teams' logos on it. The caption said "Help us solve a debate, who's gonna be the best this year?" The response was crazy. Over all of the years consulting for social media content, this single post got some of the most engagement out of all the other posts that we have ever done. Period. We got involved with what the community already loved. It was fun, lighthearted, and it worked.

Make an intentional practice with your church's Instagram profile to include a healthy balance of community-focused content. Over time, people will be much more likely to trust you with spiritual advice if they already like what you stand for.

Be strategic by being local.

LEAD PASTOR'S INSTAGRAM.

DO WE SCHEDULE THE LEAD PASTOR'S SOCIAL MEDIA TOO?

I have a surprising statistic for you. If you posted the same Instagram post on both the church's account and the lead pastor's personal account, the lead pastor's post will usually get 30% more engagement. At least. Throughout my years of overseeing the social media content for churches, I have personally tested this out. The reason is simple: people are more interested in a person than a brand. Whether you like it or not, the lead pastor's Instagram account is now a direct extension of your church.

Just like there are strategies and content schedules for the church's Instagram account, there should be the same for the lead pastor account. However, the content you post on the pastor's account should be different than what you post on the church's account. It should seem a bit more personal, with a different voice. Generally, everyone who follows the church's Instagram account will also follow the lead pastor's account. Most times they will originally follow the lead pastor only, and then later also follow the church's account. This makes the lead pastor's social media a central part of the top of the funnel. The reason the lead pastor's account is more effective in producing engagement is because it feels personal. People feel like they are getting to see a real-life look into the lead pastor's personal life. Following the lead pastor's account makes them feel like they are connected personally, and not just a consumer. This is a very important difference, and it has to be protected. If the content and voice of the lead pastor account is too similar to the church's voice, then you will lose your connection with those followers.

Every post and image that is planned for the lead pastor account should sound like it is directly from the pastor. Instead of using pronouns like "we" and "us," try to stick to using "I" and "me." Whenever possible, try to not use canned graphics or photos that were already used on the church's profile. If you are the lead pastor, and you don't personally use Instagram in your life…this is going to be a challenge for you. You probably didn't realize how important this is for your church. It is not about your desire or lack thereof to share your life on Instagram. In fact, this has nothing to do with your personal wants. The purpose of becoming active personally on Instagram is to build a deeper connection with the people in your influence. They are on social media, and you can reach them where they are at. People need to feel like they know you on a personal level before they will receive from you on a spiritual level. Don't look at this as an added job or responsibility. That is the wrong way to think of it. What you should realize is that I just opened your eyes to a powerful tool to build connection, influence, and trust. Remember, this is about reaching people.

Recently we worked with a very large church to help increase their reach and presence on social media. They specifically wanted to gain more traction on Instagram. The lead pastor of this church, let's call him Mike, was personally active on Facebook but did not have an Instagram account. After some guidance from us, the church set Mike up with his own Instagram account. Mike agreed to it, but he did not personally use it at all, even though we kept asking him to. Every post on his personal Instagram account became the same kind of content as on the main church profile, because it was only us posting. His Facebook, however, had a ton of great posts from him personally. As we tracked our engagement across both platforms, there was a huge discrepancy between the amount of engagement we got on Facebook and the amount we got on Instagram. Facebook totally dominated. Even though the content we were posting on Instagram was our best stuff each week, the Facebook content got way more likes, comments, and shares than anything on Instagram. Why is this? It is because Mike was using Facebook to share personal content.

On Facebook he would post family pictures, and share his feelings on the recent football game…typical personal content. But here's where the marketing comes in—we would add strategic content alongside his personal posts. Content about his upcoming message series and new church events. Because it was coming from his personal account, it really carried weight with his followers. With this combination, we were able to achieve huge increase in Mike's Facebook influence. In sad contrast, after only five months of posting content on Mike's Instagram, it had barely any traction, and we ended up shutting it down. It just didn't stick. It wasn't real or genuine, and people could tell it was not done with any personal involvement from Mike. This church knows that their target demographic is much more active on Instagram. They thought that publishing good content would make a following happen for Mike on Instagram, but without his personal connection, they couldn't make it launch.

Pastors, you have to dive in to Instagram personally. You just have to. It is a simple sacrifice that you can make to add people to your funnel.

So when you schedule for Instagram, remember to include great content into the lead pastor's schedule. And if you are the lead pastor, consider it part of your ministry to share snippets of your personal life on Instagram. Make it daily. People want to know you. Once they know you, the doors will open for you to influence them for good. Having your team publish content on your behalf, without the equal input of your personal posts, will fail quickly. But combine the strategic posts with your personal content, and watch the numbers skyrocket.

First people want to know you, then they want to receive from you.

SECRET SIX

UNDERSTAND
FACEBOOK.

FACEBOOK OVERVIEW.

WHAT IS THE RIGHT WAY TO USE FACEBOOK AS A CHURCH?

I love Instagram, and for now it is my go-to, but don't sleep on Facebook. If you use Facebook the right way, you will see huge impact. You just have to understand people's state of mind when they are using Facebook. It's different than Instagram, different than Snapchat, TikTok, or Twitter. Each social media platform has its own user behaviors and mindsets. Facebook also has a totally different audience demographic. Great marketers try to make their strategy unique and tailored for each social platform. They think about what kind of people are on Facebook, and what content they would want to see. There are moments every day when people at work or at home have gaps in their schedules. Little gaps when they have a second to check social media. **These gaps are where you win the battle.** Gaps between appointments, during commercials, and gaps where there shouldn't be a gap but your brain just needs a break. This is when we grab our phones and scroll through our social media platforms. Some people instinctively open Instagram, some scroll through Facebook, and many check both. The strategy to win with Facebook is different than anywhere else. It has its unique advantages and challenges, but if done right, you can gain massive amounts of interaction and depth.

Beyond mindset differences, there are some functionality differences on Facebook as well. On Facebook posts, you can include an outbound link to a website, but on Instagram you can't. I cringe when I see an Instagram post with a typed out website URL, when it is well-known that people cannot click on it. But with Facebook, you can do things like post a snippet of a recent message, a blog post, or a special event, with a direct link to that URL. Facebook will even pull some of the images and words from that URL and automatically put it into the post. You can share links to relevant news articles, inspirational videos, or even local businesses if you want. Why is this a big deal? It's because **people are much more willing to follow outbound links on Facebook than any other social media platform.** When you are on Instagram, it is difficult to get people to leave the Instagram app and visit an outbound link. They are not in that mindset. They just want to check out Instagram content. However on Facebook, people will click outbound links much more often. Knowing this should play a role in the content you post. Share articles or blog posts. Link to special events on your website. Using an outbound link on Facebook will create engagement with the post in the comments or with shares.

It is not just the mindset and functions that are different on Facebook, it is the actual people. At the core, I am a data nerd. I love analytics, charts, and even spreadsheets. Ew, I know. One thing I love about Facebook is that they give you analytics and data on your audience. If you are an admin on your church's Facebook business page, you will see an Insights button. This is a tab where you can see in-depth details about your specific audience on Facebook. In this Insights page, you can see the top locations of the people who most engage with your page, their ages, gender, and even key times of the day that they interact online. If your church is like most, you will notice that the majority of the interaction you get on Facebook is from **45- to 54-year-old females.** This is pretty common across the hundreds of churches that we have evaluated. Taking that statistic into consideration, when you are on Facebook, consider that you might get more traction if you focus your content on family happenings and posts that ask for interaction and comments. These kinds of posts perform very well with this demographic. Know who you are speaking to, and you will deepen your engagement.

When posting Facebook content, think about ways to reach the friends of your current followers. If you can tap into the influence of other people's Facebook friends, your church will get more of a social reach than you can on your own. A great way to do this is by tagging people in photos whenever possible. When you tag someone in a photo, it appears on that person's main feed and is shown to all of their friends. By doing this, many that have never been to your church will be introduced to your Facebook page just by seeing tagged photos of their friends. Another great tip is to ask your serve team, staff, and everyone you can to "check in" on Facebook on Sundays. When someone checks in on Facebook, it shows up on their feed for all of their friends to see. Many churches will put up a request on their main screens reminding people to check in because of this very reason. By the time you are reading this book, there will likely be more options like this. Use them as much as possible. Anytime you can have something about your church show up on someone's personal feed, do it. **The organic reach of content from others is as good as a personal recommendation to check out your church.**

Remember who your audience is, and what they want to see on Facebook.

FACEBOOK EVENTS.

WHAT'S THE BENEFIT OF MAKING FACEBOOK EVENTS?

Facebook events are underutilized by churches, simply because they don't understand why they are awesome. You as a church media team should go all in on Facebook events until they stop working. This means that all of your special events, your big Sundays, new message series kickoffs, and really anything that needs maximum attendance, should be made into a Facebook event. This doesn't mean that you shouldn't add the events to your website or app—you should definitely do that—just don't forget to make it a Facebook event also. Why? **Because it will reach way more people.**

When you make a Facebook event, your followers will see it just like a normal post. But here is the good stuff—when someone clicks that they are "going" to your Facebook event, their Facebook friends see it too. Facebook sometimes will even show a notification to people that says something like "Seven of your friends are attending an event near you this weekend" and it will link directly to your Facebook event. So now you have hundreds of targeted people seeing your church's event. Hundreds of people whom you would not have reached otherwise. This will really enlarge your reach and awareness.

After you have created and launched the Facebook event, then the fun begins. People can post comments, ask questions, or even share media directly on the event page itself. Now your followers have a built-in way to directly invite their friends through Facebook. This means that the invite isn't coming from you, it is coming from their personal friends, and people are more likely to come if someone they know is inviting them. Furthermore, when someone posts a comment in the Facebook event, it notifies all the followers of that event. Once you get people to click that they are "going" or "interested" on the page, you can continue to build excitement and anticipation leading up to the day of the event.

We once worked with a church that wanted to promote their upcoming VBS, and one of the main ways that we promoted it was through a really well-done Facebook event. Facebook ads allows you to directly advertise a Facebook event, so we went all in. After a bit of advertising, we got a good number of families that clicked that they were "going" to the VBS. However, we knew that we couldn't stop there. Many people who respond to a Facebook event will end up forgetting about it or not following through. We didn't want that, so we started posting fun promo videos and unique content every day on the Facebook event page. We wanted people to stay engaged and excited about the VBS. We even did a trivia giveaway that we only posted in the Facebook event page. We wanted people to stay engaged and excited about the VBS.

We ended up seeing a huge spike in attendees once we stopped assuming that everyone who clicked on "going" was actually going to come. We still had to reel them in. We decided that someone who clicked that they were "going" to the Facebook event simply meant that they were interested, but not necessarily committed. We kept engaging with them in that Facebook event all the way up to the day before the VBS started. And it worked! That year was the highest attended VBS that church has ever had, and we attribute its success to going deep with Facebook events. And one of the best parts? The church spent less advertising dollars than they had in previous years. If we had not gone with a Facebook event strategy, we would have spent more money and still not have achieved those results.

Make it part of your routine to set up and maintain Facebook events every time. You won't regret it.

FACEBOOK GROUPS.

SHOULD WE SET UP FACEBOOK GROUPS FOR OUR CHURCH?

Setting up private or public Facebook groups is a great way to create a deeper level of connectivity and engagement with your followers. When you do a post on your main Facebook page, you have to assume that you are talking to your primary church members, but also people who are just testing the waters. With a Facebook group, you can set up a page solely for established members of your church, and within that group, post more internally focused content.

Some churches set up private Facebook groups to connect different teams and departments. A church we work with has a private group set up for their "Serve Team" and there they post announcements and content specifically for that team. There is a lot of engagement that happens in that group, and it is a great way to build friendships and community. People within the volunteer team connect with each other throughout the week, and it is great. They share their prayer requests, post pictures from their ministries, and even invite each other to social events. The admins will even make a "Volunteer of the Week" post in that group and give a special thanks for that team member. A private group like this is also a place to share content that would only be appropriate for that specific audience. As an example, you could post a reminder for the team to wear their "Serve Team" shirts on Sunday. Or the lead pastor could offer some tips and encouragement specifically for this group of people. This isn't an outreach tool for marketing to new people, but it is a great way to start relationships internally at your church.

Public Facebook groups are a tool that you could use to connect with people who are new to the church. People in these groups can start to build relationships with other families and get to know people on a personal basis. We have a church in Dallas that has a public Facebook group specifically for parents. They post reminders about early check-in and upcoming kids' ministry events, and they share photos of the kids worshiping and playing together. There are parents posting about play-dates, and offering hand-me-down clothing, and so many other things that connect the parents within the church. What a great way to build relationships in your church community! You don't want people to just be attendees of your church but to have deep relationships, and deep roots are formed when people start connecting outside of Sunday services. Often the first step is for people to get to know each other in these groups. You can set these groups up as a staff and ask a volunteer to manage them.

A strategy that can also work is to create public Facebook groups that are externally focused, instead of internally focused. This means that instead of creating a Facebook group for people within your church, you create a group that anyone in your community can join. There was a church on the East Coast that had created a public Facebook group just for Christian college students. The college pastor posted frequent content to encourage students in their spiritual growth. He shared resources about upcoming events, and even reached out to students to do guest blogs. Eventually they had thousands of students join this group, and it became bigger than just what the pastor was posting. People started connecting with each other and posting helpful content. Even students who would never attend their church still found a community in this Facebook group. This was a great way to help students who were away from their families to find new friends and hopefully get plugged in at their local church.

Use Facebook groups to start lasting relationships.

LIVESTREAM VS. FACEBOOK LIVE.

SHOULD WE GO FACEBOOK LIVE FOR OUR SERVICES? OR LIVESTREAM? OR BOTH?

Facebook Live has made an incredible impact for churches. There is really no comparison between view rates on Facebook Live compared to traditional livestreaming. Facebook Live wins every time. If you aren't broadcasting your services on Facebook Live, you are one of the few. Going Facebook Live is totally different than signing up for a traditional livestream service. Most churches have actually canceled those livestream providers and now only broadcast on Facebook Live each Sunday. Why is it so different? Two words: social reach.

Connecting and interacting is so easy on Facebook Live. YouTube has a really great livestream option, but the interaction isn't as good as Facebook. Facebook will notify you when your church has gone live, so you won't miss it. And when someone is watching your Facebook Live, they can share it, comment on it, and interact directly with the church right there on the livestream. This gains views, engagement, and new followers.

However, before you decide to go live, and if your church has the resources available, you should invest into some tools and equipment to help improve your Facebook Live quality. It doesn't always have to be a separate camera for livestream only. Some churches have already invested in high-end cameras that project up on the screens in the service. You can just tap into that same feed and use it for your Facebook Live broadcast. This gives you multiple angles and high-resolution quality. For the audio, you will improve your quality if you use a separate mixer board for the live feed. If you can't afford to have a separate mixer system, then you can have your live feed come out of the same board as the main system, just with its own mix. A good method we have found is to dedicate four or five groups of inputs to a few separate channels that you mix just for your broadcast. You could, for example, send all of the drums and bass to one group, all of the other instruments and tracks to another group, vocals in a third group, and finally the lead pastor gets his or her own channel. If it is too tight to have both the Front of House (FOH) and the broadcast mixer behind the board at the same time, many contemporary digital mixers come with their own app. With an app integration, the broadcast mixer can manage their own mix from a different location in the building. This allows you to listen with ear buds and get a mix that is better suited for online streaming.

As churches progress, more people will want to focus their attention on delivering high-quality broadcasts. Soon churches will be more concerned with their livestream than their in-person experiences. It's because the online numbers will likely surpass the in-person numbers. Once you get a look at the data on your Facebook Live, you will start to see that sometimes the number of people watching online is three or four times greater than those who actually came in person. **Don't fight it—you won't win.** Instead, make your entire Facebook Live experience excellent. Don't just throw up any old raw footage, because this is the first impression a lot of people will get for your church. When your livestream is excellent, then you will start to reach more viewers than ever before.

One church in Atlanta that we work with has a very large online following. Their Facebook Live usually has well over 2,000 viewers throughout the service. Each Sunday they have a specific volunteer whose job is to engage with everyone within the comments. This person introduces him/herself to all of the people who join the Facebook Live, chats with them, and posts comments throughout the service. Over years of doing this, it has been a positive first impression for people. **The livestream on Facebook is part of the top of your funnel.** You should expect that most people watching are just testing the waters. Greeting them with a friendly introduction is a great way to build relationship and draw them in.

So don't just worry about the service in your Facebook Live, but learn from our church in Atlanta and make the whole experience interactive. Dedicate an individual or small team whose sole job is to produce the Facebook Live. Train them. Resource them. This is a big deal. Trust me, I know this sounds intense, and you don't need yet another task on your plate. But the numbers don't lie. These are real people who are ready to connect with your church, so make their experience an excellent one. The Facebook Live team can put together a five minute prerecorded video or live program before the beginning of the service each week to hook people in and get them to join the livestream. They can share announcements, do fun interviews, or strictly engage with people during this pre-service video. The team is also responsible for engaging with comments and interactions on the feed before and during the service, being a friendly and welcoming voice to any newcomer.

And finally, at the end of your Facebook Live, there should be a conclusion with a call to action like prayer requests, small group registration, or online giving. It does sound like a lot of work, and it is. However, when you think strictly about the numbers, this small Facebook Live team could be making an impactful experience for sometimes double or triple the number of people who came in person.

The numbers don't lie: Facebook Live will be your biggest audience.

DEALING WITH COMMENTS AND MESSAGES.

SO WAIT, I HAVE TO ACTUALLY BE SOCIAL ON OUR SOCIAL MEDIA?

Recently we ran an ad campaign for fifty different churches around Thanksgiving. We created a post discussing about how the holidays can be a hard time for some people, and that we wanted to know how we could pray for them. The call to action was to send the church a message so they could pray for and encourage them. Our goal was to build some new relationships with people in the community and to help anyone who was in a difficult season. I was pleasantly surprised at how many responses we were able to generate. We were seeing anywhere between seven to twenty direct messages (DMs) on Facebook and Instagram per week, and they were really sincere messages asking for prayer. What an awesome opportunity to help bring encouragement to people and build relationships, right? When our team was monitoring the results of this Facebook ad, I found out some terrible news. Churches were not responding to, or even reading most of the messages. I was so mad! These churches were literally running an ad asking people how they could pray for them during a difficult season, and then they turned around and ignored the responses. **Not cool.** There were people leaving genuine comments on the posts or sending DMs asking for prayer, and they would get no reply. Some churches had a Facebook auto responder on, but this almost made it worse because it said that someone would get back to them shortly, which was also not true. Eventually, we got all of the churches to start responding, but it wouldn't have happened if we did not push for it. These could have been missed opportunities, leaving people offended and hurt and with a great distaste for the church.

Make it a hard rule. Everyone gets a response when they comment or message you on Facebook. Period. Social media works so much better when people feel like they are actually interacting with someone, instead of just consuming your content. In fact, you should post content on your Facebook feed sometimes that specifically asks a question, purely for engagement. Perhaps you have heard of Facebook's algorithm: they intentionally show content to more people if the post is already getting engagement. Why? Because Facebook wants to have their users enjoy their experience, and the way they determine what posts to show is by how many comments and interactions that post receives. And it's not just about that one post; they actually factor in how much engagement your page gets in general. You want to protect your engagement ranking by being very responsive to everyone who interacts with you. Frequently create engagement posts that ask a question, like "Who's got great plans this weekend?" or something like that. When you get a comment under that post, respond to that person directly in the thread. It can be as simple as hitting the Like button on their comment, or you can actually write a response back. This matters not only because of the algorithm, but also because it sets a precedence that when people engage with you, someone is actually going to interact with them. Your social media feels organic when you put in the time to actually respond on a human-to-human level.

However, you don't always have to wait for them to leave a comment. If you are really serious about connecting with someone, you can reach out directly to them. There is a church we work with in Florida who sends personal, non-automated DMs to tons of people who like or comment on their social media posts. Wait what? Now that's just crazy. **But maybe crazy might just work.** Through these messages, the church introduces themselves and personally invites people to an upcoming service. These are completely individualized messages, sent out one by one. This church has many members today who actually first came simply because of that one DM. A great strategy to set up is to do an ad or a boost that is shown to people who are in your local area, but in that post, the custom audience is set up to exclude people who already "like" or follow your church's page. The purpose of narrowing your audience like this is so you can assume that all of the interaction on the post is from someone who is not already a member of your church. That's a pretty dialed-in audience to send these messages to and invite to your next service or big day!

There are two schools of thought when it comes to marketing, and they both work. One is the shotgun approach, and one is the sniper approach. The shotgun approach is where you take your message and blast it to a wide range of people, showing it to as many people as you can...but you don't really know what kind of results you will get, like a shotgun blast. The sniper method is when you focus on a single individual at a time and spend your energy on that one person. Like a sniper takes time to aim and shoot at his/her targets one by one. Both strategies have their benefits. Going one by one works with churches because people appreciate the personal connection and feel more compelled to take the next step, but a shotgun approach can often reach a higher volume of people. You just have to see what works best for you.

Trust me, I know how spread thin you can get in ministry. Spending time each day responding to comments and messages on Facebook is probably not always going to fit into your schedule. But if you really want to use Facebook as a means to build new connections and relationships, this simply has to be a priority. **So ask for help.** Have select staff members or volunteers install the Facebook Pages app and turn on notifications for comments and messages for your church's page. Make it a team effort. If you can have at least three or four people with the responsibility to make sure that comments and messages get a quick response, then you should be set.

People want to talk with people, not bots.

SECRET SEVEN

THE PERFECT CHURCH WEBSITE.

WEBSITE OVERVIEW.

DOES OUR CHURCH WEBSITE NEED HELP?

Most pastors would love to have an amazing website. One that has all the bells and whistles, and more importantly, one that gets people in the doors on Sunday! But most people don't have a full-time web developer on staff, nor do they have $15k to drop on a custom-built website. We have had years of experience developing completely custom websites for churches all over the world. With this experience I have been able to identify some areas that can really make or break a church website.

First things first. Who is your website built for? Yes, there are key pages on your website that your current church members need to use. They will want to register for events, give online, or even listen to messages that they missed. But primarily your church's website is a tool for reaching people who don't already attend. People who don't know Jesus. You should be speaking to the non-member when choosing the hierarchy of information, the colors, and the calls to action. Every decision regarding page order, content, and verbiage needs to be pointed towards reaching the lost and those seeking a new church home.

My family and I live on the Central Coast of California. When we first moved here, we knew that we needed to find a church family. What was my first step? I got out my iPhone and did a quick Google search for churches in the area. There were seven or eight results that seemed like a potential fit, so I pulled up each of their websites to check them out. Some of the websites looked like they were built fifteen years ago, which gave the vibe that those churches were totally outdated. Some of the church sites didn't even work well on my phone, so I couldn't really see much about them. And some of the websites took so long to load that I just gave up on them.

We did eventually find a church online that seemed pretty good. We visited for a few weeks, and really enjoyed it! We had found our new church. I was very glad we found it, and quite thankful that their website gave us such a good first impression. If it had not, we may have never attended. We didn't have friends in the area at the time, so searching online was really the only way that we knew how to check out our options. The truth is, I probably missed out on some great churches by only making my judgment based on their websites. I know that. But how many other people were turned away because of their bad websites too? You have to assume that many other people will go through the same exact process that we did when they are looking for a church. This is why your website is a big deal.

Today is different than it used to be, and now first impressions happen online, not when people just show up on a Sunday morning for the first time. That rarely happens. If you are not careful, you could have a first impression of your church that makes you seem unprofessional and sloppy, simply because of your website. This is why it matters. The scary thing is, you can't measure how many people you miss out on because of your website. All of those six or seven churches that I didn't visit will never know. There is no box to check or metric to read about how many people were ready to visit, but then were turned off by your website. This is serious business. In this chapter, I am going to give you the knowledge you need to ensure that you don't miss out on new visitors like those local churches did.

Your church's website is worth the investment.

CUSTOM VS. TEMPLATE.

HOW DO I CHOOSE THE RIGHT WEBSITE PROVIDER?

There are tons of options when it comes to websites. It can be exhausting to try and understand them all, but don't worry, because that's where I come in. When most churches are starting out, they certainly would love to have a big, fancy, custom-built website that is designed by pros. But that is usually out of reach. A fully custom designed and developed website will range in cost from $10,000 to $20,000 depending on how large it is. This is completely out of the question for most churches. So what do they do? The next best option is to settle for using a website template builder program like Squarespace or Wix, or some Christian spin-off version. These programs have pre-built templates where you can just add your own words and photos. Sometimes this is sufficient for a smaller-sized church just starting out. However, keep in mind that with template programs like this, you can't add things that are outside of the template restrictions. This means that you won't have much freedom in the way your site is laid out. If you are like me, this is a big problem. I want my site to be the best it can possibly be, because I know how serious of a deal this is.

For the many churches who need to have a professional website, these template sites won't be the way to go. But for churches who are just getting started and don't have the extra budget, templates are a really good option. I suggest Squarespace to get started. It doesn't have a huge learning curve, and you can get it up and running for around $20/month. As someone who markets and designs websites for churches for a living, I will always prefer custom-built websites over templates, but I want you to know that sometimes using a cheaper template will get the job done in the beginning phases of your church. Once you grow and your budget allows for it, you can redo your website with a custom designer.

If you do have the ability to redo your church's website, you are going to want to make sure it is done right. Let's start by talking about the design. The design is the most important part, so have a professional do it. You can assume that almost 100% of all first-time guests who visit your church have probably already checked you out online, thus your website is a big deal—you only get one shot at their first impression.

When having your website designed, think beyond just how attractive and fun it looks. **You need to be strategic with the layout and calls to action.** You can do things like adding unique pop ups, having an interactive Bible reading plan, creatively embedding your Instagram feed, or presenting your core values in a particular way. You can even have your website integrate directly with your database for events, registrations, online giving, and contact forms. Instruct your web designer to incorporate subtle animations and movement into your site that will really bring things to life.

We developed a website recently for a church in San Francisco that had a lot of unique features in it. We added some playful elements where certain parts of a picture would appear blurry until you put your mouse over it, and then it would appear focused. And there were hidden triggers, where if you put your mouse over a certain part of a photo, a different video would appear. It wasn't necessary, but it just added to an overall sense of excellence and uniqueness. It will be up to you and your team to think creatively and push the boundaries. Your website has succeeded if you can leave people feeling a sense of who you are, and they are compelled to take the next step.

Since custom website design is out of reach for some churches right now, there are still ways to make your template-built website have a sense of wow. Use b-roll style video clips in the background of the top of your home page to really bring it to life. And make sure that you only use high-quality images that fit with the colors and style of your branding. Be sure to explore the different font type options that your template gives you, and choose one that most closely matches your church's brand guidelines as discussed earlier in this book. Most importantly, make sure you keep things up to date. Have a system where your latest messages are added to the site right after church each Sunday. Always keep it fresh. Make sure events on your website are current, and update your website with each message series to include the new series design.

When it is about the first impression, it should be a first priority.

MOBILE FIRST DESIGN.

OUR WEBSITE WORKS FINE ON MOBILE, RIGHT?

You already know that your website has to look good on a mobile device, but it is way deeper than that. After studying the analytics from hundreds of church websites, we learned just how important the mobile design of your site is. The average church receives over 80% of their monthly online traffic from a mobile device. Not a laptop or desktop. Over 80%! **That is a huge number.** There are so many more visitors from mobile phones than from other devices, so it is a must to rethink the design of your site. You should treat your website almost like you were designing a smartphone app.

Think of it like Instagram. Yes, you can technically pull up Instagram on a desktop…but what kind of weirdo would do that? The whole Instagram experience is built for a phone. The designers of Instagram first created an awesome app, and then made it work on a desktop. They went mobile first because they knew that almost everyone would be experiencing Instagram from their phones.

Imagine if we treated our church website with that same

level of detail for the mobile design! Most churches created their website primarily for a desktop, and then adjusted and resized it to fit on a mobile screen. If that's you, then you are thinking about this whole thing the wrong way. If you were designing an app for your church, you would spend all of your time thinking about the mobile experience. So with statistics showing that at least 80% of your web traffic will be from mobile, it's time to treat your church's website design more like an app than a website. **The primary design of your website is for the mobile experience,** and then you make sure that it looks good on a desktop as well. Mobile should never be an afterthought.

A term that many web companies use is "responsive" website designs. If your web developer tells you that your site will be responsive, you might want to clarify exactly what they mean by that. The old way of building responsive websites was to design the entire page for a desktop, and then depending on the user's screen size, it would automatically restack the different elements on that page so that everything would fit. This is not the most ideal way to have your website built anymore. When the content and layout is primarily designed for the screen size of a desktop, there is usually too much content to fit onto a phone screen. People on phones are tired of scrolling for five minutes just to get to the bottom of a page. People on phones are tired of having to scroll back to the top of the screen just to reach the menu. **People on phones are tired of having to wait nineteen minutes for your website to load.** This is 80% of your audience, and if you don't fix your website, you are going to lose your chance to meet these new people face to face.

Top web development agencies create completely separate versions of the website specifically for mobile-, tablet-, and desktop- sized screens. **Each version has a totally different design.** This allows you to have a mobile design that operates similar to an app, instead of just being a resized desktop site. You can choose to have content like your beliefs, core values, or anything that is text-heavy to be split up into toggled sections. You can have your message player operate more like a podcast, and you can even have your menu on the bottom of the screen as seen on apps like Facebook and Instagram. The possibilities are endless.

Tell your creative team to **think first of the mobile experience** when coming up with ideas for your website.

CHURCH APPS.

DO WE NEED TO GET A CHURCH APP?

I probably get asked about the importance of a church app around ten times a week from church leaders. Everyone has his or her own opinion about it. Sometimes having an app just because you want to is totally fine! But is it worth the financial investment? Let's talk about it.

Just like with websites, there are two main worlds when it comes to app development: custom vs. templates. If you have a custom app created for your church, it will have capabilities and styling specifically built for you. You can have functions unique to each ministry, enable users to play an active part with the Sunday experience, and even have an interactive campus map. It would be awesome! However, the development for an app like this will have a starting cost of over $70,000, and it will take at least a year to develop. Not to mention the costs for ongoing maintenance and support. If you can afford this, you will see a high usage volume on the app, and it will become a central part of your ministry organization and communication. But will it be worth the investment? I would say probably not.

Who's got $70,000 to drop on an app right now? Not many. Until app development becomes more affordable, it isn't the right time to have a truly custom-built app. So the alternative option is to use an app provider that has a pre-built template. Lots of online giving providers will actually throw in a templated app as an incentive to sign up with them. The primary things that people use template-based apps for are giving, online messages, and possibly event registration. **But keep in mind that you can already do all of this on your website.** So the issue with template-based apps is that there essentially is no difference between the app and your website.

There is only one differentiating factor—push notifications. You can only do that with an app. Although this sounds like a big deal, I have found that it is very rare that churches actually continuously use push notifications through their app. It takes a lot of upkeep to do it right, and people usually don't have time for that. It is just not as useful as it sounds in an ongoing, regular basis. If your church is one that uses it and really finds benefit, that is great, but the majority of churches would be better off leaving the app idea outside and focusing instead on their websites.

So put your effort into making the mobile design of your website amazing, instead of adding a template-based app. Your app will become an additional item on your to-do list for maintenance and updating, and you probably don't need that.

Template apps are overrated. Let your website do its job.

THE PERFECT HOME PAGE.

DO WE HAVE THE RIGHT MESSAGE ON OUR HOME PAGE?

Let's talk about what to talk about. Your website is filled with words and messages—a lot of information that obviously needs to be communicated. Things like your beliefs, contact information, event announcements…the basics. But you must be sure that your voice and message speaks to the right person.

Saying things in the right order matters a lot. Don't just think about what looks pretty. Most church websites have way too much information on the first few sections of the home page that is totally irrelevant to a first-time guest. They have information about their upcoming VBS, their serve team, and other sections that are internal. Since you are putting valuable time and resources into the funnel that drives seekers to your website, make your website primarily focus on converting people into the next phase of the funnel. The internal information should be there, but not featured on the home page.

In sales you are taught to have a clear call to action on your website, and it has to repeat on every page. Always make it obvious to the user. In the marketing industry, professionals have found that people need to know immediately what you want them to do, or they won't do it. You must never assume that people will know what the call to action is. Take the test: when you open your website, would you know what your next step is within the first few seconds? **If users have to search for it, they won't.**

Your website is not a scrapbook of pretty videos and pictures about your church. It's a tool for reaching people. Remember its purpose, and you will make the right decisions with its hierarchy of information. Decide what it is that you want people to do. **What is your call to action?** It has to be one of the first things that people see. Some churches have a button that says "Join Us" or "Plan Your Visit" or even "Watch Latest Message" as their call to action. Each of these work. It simply depends on what your goal is. However, if you are using the funnel, then your call to action should probably be "Plan Your Visit" or something similar. Before understanding what I know now, I have been guilty of designing church websites with way too much irrelevant content on the home page. But never again, because now I know who it is that I am building that web page for. People visit your website's home page who don't know Jesus, don't know what church life is about, and they are hesitant about the whole thing. But they know they have a need, and they are looking. This is who your website is primarily built for. **This is the why.**

Too many calls to action will hurt you. One or two should be the maximum. I have seen some churches have a Plan Your Visit button, and then a Give Now button, and then a Join A Group button, and then a Watch Online button...the list goes on. That is too many. The user needs to know what the main ask is. **Once you know what your clear call to action is, make sure that it is on every page.**

The top of the home page is the first thing that most people will see, so put the call to action there. You should also have your main headline on the top as well. A great main headline is one that starts the user on a thought process. It is different than simply putting your church name; it is a sentence or two that immediately speaks to the user. In marketing, this spot on the website is called "above the fold" placement. This term actually originated in the newspaper industry. It was crucial for newspaper editors to put a headline above the main middle fold of the paper that people would see when going by newsstands. It was a strategy to sell more papers with a compelling headline that people would want to read. In the land of e-commerce, above the fold now refers to what people see before they scroll, both on mobile and desktop. Make the headline and call to action enticing and clear, before people even have to scroll down to see more.

This definitely applies to your church's website. The headline on the top of your home page, before you have to scroll, must be strategic and compelling. Some people put their mission statement or their tagline here. This is a great start, but you could do even better. Our team analyzes the behavior on hundreds of church websites each month and we found a surprising pattern. **Around 75% of all website traffic to a church's site never leaves the home page of the website.** They get the general idea from the first page, and that's as far as they go. They don't go to the About page, they don't visit the I'm New page, they don't go anywhere but the home page. We also found that the average time spent on a church website is less than four minutes. What does this tell us? That for 75% of the people who visit your website, you only have four minutes or less, and only one page, to tell the story you want to tell. This is a challenge. You can't waste any space on your home page speaking to anything other than the main goal, which is to move them along in the funnel. **Let your main thing, be your main thing.**

Take people on a journey as they scroll down your home page. Give people the questions and the answers. People best consume ideas in sets of threes. There should be three steps in the home page journey, and no more than three. **These are the three questions that you should answer: Who are you? Why does it matter? What should they do next?** Who are you is where your main headline goes. Make your headline enticing so people are curious enough to keep scrolling. Here are some samples that give you an idea of what would work:

Your life is about to change.

Orlando will never be the same.

Are you ready for something different?

The next step is the why it matters section. This is where your mission statement and core values section are explored. Talk about how much you love your city or how your church changes lives. Let people know that there is a purpose behind your church. People want to be a part of something that is bigger than themselves. The primary call to action should be repeated in this section as well, but you can add a secondary one if you would like. A great example of this would be if you choose the headline of "Your life is about to change" on the top, you could title this section "Take the first step" and have supporting content plus your main call to action button. A good example of a secondary call to action would be a Latest Message button which directs the user to the messages page.

The final section is the Plan Your Visit or the call to action section. Although the call to action is also in the headline section of your site, it needs its own section on your home page that offers some further explanation to the process. Let them know why they should take this call to action, and walk them through the process.

Obviously you need to prayerfully decide what your call to action is and what the three steps are for your church. But if you can stick to this model you will find that the 75% of people who only visit your home page will now know exactly what you are, why you exist, and what to do next. Certainly in the main menu you need to have links to all of the other pages on your website, but the home page should be devoted to the seeker. The funnel is built for them. Resist the temptation to go beyond the three-step approach, and make sure your headlines are clear and enticing.

Remember who your website is for, and the rest will fall into place.

I'M NEW & PLAN YOUR VISIT.

WHAT IS THE PERFECT PAGE FOR FIRST-TIME GUESTS?

While the home page is the main section for reaching new people, the second most important page on your church's website is the "Plan Your Visit" page. There are many different names that you can use for this page like "I'm New" or "My First Time," but the purpose is the same. **This page is crucial because it should be the primary call to action throughout your entire website.** The main button on the home page, and every other page, should lead guests back to this page. Spend just as much time thinking through the design and layout of this page as you did your home page.

There has been a huge explosion in popularity in the past three or four years in the use of a Plan Your Visit page for churches. Plan Your Visit is a contact form that people can fill out in advance for their first visit at your church. If they fill out this Plan Your Visit contact form, they are offered some resources, early childcare check in, and/or a personalized experience during their first visit. Churches have had a ton of success with this model, so some literally have a Plan Your Visit pop up on every page of the website. I don't recommend going that far with it, but I have found that a Plan Your Visit form does work. It works best when used with the funnel so people are already primed for an ask.

The churches that have the most success with Plan Your Visit forms have a clear and compelling reason why someone should fill out the form. There are too many churches who have a Plan Your Visit page that asks the user to fill out a contact form with little to no explanation of why they should fill it out. If you want this to work well, you need to clearly describe what will happen after they fill out the form. All of your funnel marketing has lead up to this big ask, so give them a convincing reason why they should fill it out. Tell them that they will get a personal experience, or text message, or something. **Make it clear, and make it attractive.**

Here is a bold idea that our team was the first to invent. Everybody has some sort of welcome gift in their church, right? You could actually allow someone to set up a personalized welcome gift using the Plan Your Visit form. Imagine being invited to come to a church for the first time, and you could actually pick what you wanted in your own welcome basket. For example, step one on the Plan Your Visit page would be to pick if you want a red t-shirt or a black one. Then pick your size. Then you would pick if you want a coffee cup or a notepad with the church logo on it. The point is, visitors get to customize a few options. Then someone puts it together for them before the weekend service, and writes them a welcome note. How cool is that? Now potential visitors have a compelling reason why they should fill out this form, because they get free stuff that they picked out.

But wait, there's more! Saturday night, this person is going to have second thoughts about waking up early and going to church. You know how it is. But when they remember that someone has personally put together a whole gift basket just for them, they would feel terrible if they just didn't show up. So even if they have second thoughts, they feel obligated to come, and boom—now you have increased your conversion rate. You can thank me later for this golden nugget!

But as great as it is, you can't stop with just a contact form. You need to have an organized system for incoming Plan Your Visit forms. You should have a team with an exact procedure of what will happen as soon as someone fills out that form. One of the churches that we work with in Seattle has an entire strategic system involving multiple volunteers for every Plan Your Visit form they receive. It is really awesome. With this church's program, once someone fills out a Plan Your Visit form, the Guest Experience Leader gets an automatic text message alert. The Guest Experience Leader is notified by text message so they can reach out quickly, even if they are away from their computer. The guest will also get a text message notifying them that they are confirmed for their upcoming visit, and that someone will be reaching out to them very shortly. The church's Guest Experience Leader sends a personal email and text message on Saturday (using a dedicated church phone number) welcoming them to church, and letting them know where to park on Sunday. It might sound like a lot, but if you keep it casual like this church does, it will be a really cool experience for the guest. The morning of the service, they get another text letting them know that a team member will be wearing a red "Serve Team" shirt and will be waiting for them under the red "Visitor" sign in the lobby. Once they meet each other, the visitor gets a personal campus tour so they know where the kids' areas are, and where to find the bathrooms and the main sanctuary. They will also be given their first-time guest gift and introduced to some church leaders. After church is over, they have a follow-up system in place as well. This church has an awesome experience for the people who use the Plan Your Visit form, and since they clearly explain this whole process on the website, they get way more form conversions than most churches. Make it clear why people should plan their visit using this page, and make the entire experience an awesome one, so you can have the same kind of results at your church.

Here are the three key sections that must be on your Plan Your Visit page: first, clearly list your service times and location, including a street map. You would be surprised at how many churches actually make this hard to find. Make sure your page mentions parking instructions, along with a map of the church campus, if you have one. Second, give an overview of what the service will be like, including a Frequently Asked Questions section that answers questions about length of service, denomination, dress type, and worship style. Finally, dedicate a section to your kids' ministry. Parents want to know what your kids' facilities are like, what your children's ministry programming is, and what age groups are offered. Make sure to have great photos of your kids' facilities along with action shots of happy kids and volunteers. You may have a Kids' Ministry page on your website, but it should also have its own section on the Plan Your Visit page.

Many churches film a short video specifically for the Plan Your Visit page on their website. These videos get incredibly high view rates, and they work wonderfully. Have the lead pastor or someone else who is the face of the Guest Experience department film the video, speaking directly to a first-time guest. Show short, b-roll style clips of the teaching, worship, and various Sunday ministries. This video tells the viewer what they can expect on a Sunday, and talks them through the process once they fill out the Plan Your Visit form. It is important that this video is really high quality. This video is for potential new guests, and the last thing you want to do is have a low-quality representation of what Sundays are like at your church.

Your Plan Your Visit page—done well—could lead to a visitor this Sunday.

Pro Tip - For the best Plan Your Visit results, use a contact form that only asks for one bit of information at a time. When people see a long contact form that asks for their first name, last name, email, phone number, number of kids coming…the form looks too long. People don't want to give you all of that information, and they might not fill out the form. You will see an increase in Plan Your Visit forms if you just ask for one bit at a time. Build your contact form to start by having visitors enter their names, and then they hit Next. A new field then appears and it asks for the date they want to come, and on it goes. Once the person has gotten three or four questions in, they usually will just finish it out. So have your contact form load one section at a time, because it really improves conversion rates. Since the person did not see a list of seven different fields to fill out initially, they are more likely to complete it.

WEBSITE LOAD SPEED.

HOW DO I MAKE OUR SITE LOAD FASTER?

If your website takes too long to load, you will lose tons of website visitors every month. When our team analyzes the performance of a website, one of the first stats we look at is called "bounce rate." This is a web analytic term that refers to the percentage of people who visit your website but leave immediately. As in less than five seconds. You certainly don't want to have a high bounce rate, because that means people are leaving your site before they even see it. They never even consume the content of your home page because they leave right away.

Why does this happen, and how do you fix it?

There are going to be bounce sessions every day on your website, and that is totally expected. If you are seeing a bounce rate somewhere between 20% and 30% you are actually in the normal range. Some people click on a link by accident, or change their minds—there are many reasons why you will have some bounce sessions. They are simply unavoidable. However, one of the main and most concerning reasons for a high bounce rate is when the user wanted to view your website, but it took too long to load, so they gave up. This is especially terrible if you are paying for ads to drive people to your site, then you lose them before they even see it. The worst part is that a high bounce rate is totally preventable. You just have to care enough to fix it.

When we test a church website's load speed, the average time is four to five seconds on desktop, and six to seven seconds on mobile. This doesn't sound like a big deal, right? Wrong. In the corporate world, this would never be acceptable. They would know they are losing thousands of dollars because of a high bounce rate. The standard that is agreed upon by most industries is a three-second load speed, both on mobile and on desktop. I know that seems fast, but anything longer than that and you will see a drastic increase in your bounce rate. Remember, **every second counts.**

I am obsessed with getting load speed right, because I know that people on their phones simply do not have patience. We know that 80% of web traffic comes from mobile, so you have to consider how people think when they are on a mobile device. It's different than when you are browsing on a desktop. When you are on your phone, you are usually using apps or browsing social media, and we get used to scrolling through photos and videos at a high speed. I literally get irritated when I click on a Facebook video and it makes me wait ten seconds as it buffers. It actually makes me mad. I assume the same goes for anyone when they have just a few minutes to be on social media. They want it fast. When your website takes longer than three seconds to load, the user simply leaves and continues on with their day. Certainly this is not the case for everyone, but when you start seeing bounce rates of 40% and higher, you know there is a problem.

The biggest culprit for a slow website is large media. When

my company creates websites, we have a rule that no images can go on a site unless they are smaller than 200kb in size. When we analyze other churches' websites, it is very common to see images that are upwards of 2mb or larger. **This will kill your load speed.**

Photos are a problem, and videos are even worse. It's popular for churches to have looping b-roll video footage in the background of the home page of their site. I love this because it really looks great when it is done right. But if your website has video footage like that, find a way to keep the video file size under 30mb if possible, otherwise it will take forever to load. If your video is larger than 30mb, there are a few things you can do. You can start by shortening the video—there is no need to have a looping video last any longer than forty-five seconds. Secondly you can use the Adobe program called Adobe Media Encoder to compress the video. Using this tool, you can reduce the size of the video by 70% or more, without noticeably losing quality.

Some churches try to use an embedded YouTube or Vimeo link in the background of their home page. Don't do that. The YouTube branding cheapens the look of the home page. However, I do find it helpful to embed other videos on your site from YouTube, just remember—not the background videos on your home page. Sections like a welcome video on the Plan Your Visit page or any videos connected to special events or announcements are great to embed from YouTube. Anything that is not used as a background element should be hosted in YouTube to help increase load speeds.

Another huge way to speed up your site is to use caching. Caching is when your website doesn't have to load the entire content of each page every time it is opened. Some of the site is preloaded so the user can view the site faster. Sounds complicated, but it's not, and it will make your site load as much as 50% faster. If you are using a template-based website, you probably won't have any options to add caching on your site. However, if you have a custom site, or are using a program like WordPress, then you can add caching. Add a caching plugin from the WordPress plugin library and play with the settings until you are pleased with the load speed. You can also call your website hosting provider and ask if they can add caching directly on the server of your website. Most caching plugins also have a functionality called "lazy loading," which is a term that refers to the way your images load. This really helps with your load speed because it only loads images one at a time instead of making them load all at once. This could take off one or two additional seconds of your load speed, which is huge.

Your site might be perfect, but if it takes too long to load, people won't stick around to see it.

Pro Tip - Do a Google search for "test my website speed" and type in your church's URL. You will get instant data on the performance of your load speed on both mobile and desktop.

PODCASTING DONE RIGHT.

HOW DO WE MAXIMIZE OUR CHURCH'S PODCAST?

It seems like almost every church has their own podcast. My advice: if you are going to do a podcast, do it with excellence. The vast majority of churches simply put the audio of their message onto their podcast, and that's it. I think you could go a step above and beyond that. Making your podcast actually feel like a podcast won't take much effort or time, but it will be a much better product in the end.

First of all, if you need to set up your podcast for the first time, here's how to do it. You will need to start with some sort of podcast hosting subscription. There are a few good ones out there to choose from. Most churches use either Podbean or Blubrry to integrate with their church website for their podcast audio. If you sign up with Blubrry, they will give you a plugin to add to your website which will create the podcast episode and RSS feed for you.

To make a podcast channel, you need to set up an admin account on Apple Podcasts, Stitcher, and wherever else you want your podcast to be distributed. Each of these podcast players will need you to paste in something called an RSS feed. An RSS feed is a URL from your website, which the podcast player receives the media and description from. Apple Podcasts (and any other podcast player) is the middleman between the media on your website and the end listener. With this RSS feed, any time you add more audio to your website, it will automatically update all of the podcast players at once.

Most churches just use the Sunday messages as the content for their podcasts and post one new podcast episode per week. This is the most common way to do church podcasts, and it works great. But here is how you do it with excellence: each week, before publishing the audio, your team should first add a compressor to the audio which makes the volume more balanced and crisp. If you want to have that professional podcast sound, the compressor is the most important tool. Next add a filter on the audio channel called a "high pass filter." This cuts out all of the very low frequencies which make the audio muddy and unclear. The high pass filter only lets the higher frequencies through, which are needed for a crisp speaking audio quality. You can easily add audio effects and settings like this using the Adobe program called Audition. Try it out, and you will immediately hear the difference.

But let's not stop there. If you really want to present your podcast messages in a highly professional way, add an intro to the podcast each week. Almost all of the top podcasts in the world use a consistent intro that is professionally done and is the same from episode to episode (although most podcasts update their intro around one to two times per year to keep it fresh). Keep your intro very short—under thirty seconds is ideal. The best intros have some background music and the voice of the lead pastor welcoming the listeners. If you don't feel comfortable recording your own intro, you could easily outsource it with a company like Upwork for less than $100. They will do a voice-over and add background music for you. It's a worthwhile investment, just as putting a little time and effort into making your podcast look and sound great is also worthwhile.

If you are going to have a podcast, make it excellent.

SECRET EIGHT

FACEBOOK & INSTAGRAM ADS.

ADS OVERVIEW.

WHY DOES IT HAVE TO BE SO COMPLICATED?

I speak with hundreds of church leaders every year, and they all say the same thing. It's some version of "Ross, I know we need to do a better job with ads on social media and Google and all that…but we really don't know how to do it." I am glad they want to be sure it is done right, and I am always happy to help, because the world of Facebook and Instagram ads is a great way to lose money if you don't know what you are doing.

When I speak to the social media manager at a church about paid ads, most people tell me that they boost posts for their ads. Some people have even set up some custom audiences and use the actual Facebook Business Manager tools. This is a great start! And that might be as far as you have gotten, but we are going to go deeper than that. When you are first starting out with paid ads on social media, it is intimidating. Trying to figure out the structure will take some time. The interface is not very user friendly, and the terms and layout are all new. It's a challenge at first, to say the least, but if it were easy, then everyone would be a great marketer. If you will invest the time and energy to really learn Facebook and Instagram ads, you will not regret it. Slow down and read this chapter carefully, **because this is the single most effective marketing tool for reaching new people that currently exists.** I promise you this; it is worth the effort of learning how to use social media ads.

Our team has had years of hands-on practice figuring out

what the perfect system is for paid ads for churches. We have designed thousands of church marketing funnels, so we have had the chance to experiment on many different types of ad strategies. With this experience, we have learned the exact system that produces results with Facebook and Instagram ads. Take your time, and after you are done reading this chapter, put it into practice right away while the information is fresh.

When I first started working with paid ads, it was surprising how different it was from managing the content on social media. **Paid ads and creative social posts are much more different than they are alike.** In our agency, I would do everything I could to teach our social media content managers about paid ads. It was brutal. As much as they wanted to learn, paid ads use a totally different part of the brain, and it is hard to get into that mode. Eventually our content creators became great at putting together ads, it just took some stretching and learning. Now, we've adapted. We have separate staff members who are completely responsible for paid ads and don't manage the creative content at all. It works so much better. It is hard for creative brains to shift over to data and analytical thinking at the same time. Most people are surprised by this contrast. It seems normal that people who specialize in Facebook and Instagram content would automatically be able to run ads on the same platform. They totally can, but it will take hard work.

If you are ready to take the challenge, this chapter is for you. With a little bit of grit and the instructions laid out in this chapter, you will finally understand paid ads and use them to reach new people. This chapter will give you in-depth instruction on all the tools at your disposal with Facebook and Instagram paid ads. There are likely more than you knew existed. Use these new skills to build your funnel and reach new people like you never have before.

SET YOUR BUDGET.

HOW MUCH MONEY SHOULD WE SPEND ON SOCIAL MEDIA ADS?

Most churches are not chomping at the bit to spend money on marketing. In fact, a lack of budget is the primary reason people don't run ad campaigns. I get it. But marketing is a must, and once you start seeing steady growth with your funnel, you will realize that it was worth the investment.

But how much should you be spending? Most people aren't thinking the right way about a marketing budget. When I have the budget talk with church leaders, most of the time they tell me a figure like, "We want to spend $700 for our VBS this year," or something like that. They give me a flat figure for that specific event. That is a good start. Dedicating a separate marketing budget for special events is important, but that isn't how the funnel works. **The funnel is ongoing and never stops.** You need to set aside a recurring monthly budget for your funnel marketing. It is not a one-time figure; it is ongoing. Your funnel budget is a dedicated amount that you spend every single month.

Now that we've got that settled, how much should you spend each month? I fully understand that every church has different budget limitations, so these figures are suggestions based on the marketing campaigns we have set up for hundreds of churches of various sizes. Below is a list of suggested monthly advertising budgets broken down by church size:

$300/month: 0-100 member church
$500/month: 100-500 member church
$750/month: 500-1,000 member church
$1,500/month: 1,000-1,500 member church
$2,000/month: 1,500+ member church

Some of you just lost your mind reading those numbers. You think I'm nuts! I get that. So, for those of you who just fell out of your chairs, please stay with me. Some of you reading this book might actually be spending more than these amounts already, and you think I'm under budget. But if your ads are done according to the funnel systems laid out in this book, you will be able to stay right in this budget range and receive great results. So there, I just saved you money! But whether you think this budget is too much or not enough, here is the news that is really going to make some of you mad at me—and feel free to throw this book against the wall after you read this—this budget is only for social media ads. This does not include Google Ads. Google Ads are a part of the top of the funnel strategy, and we will be diving more into that later in this book.

Once you have accepted the monthly budget, you need to make sure that you spread it correctly between the top and middle of the funnel. The top of your funnel should receive 80% of your budget. The remaining 20% is dedicated for retargeting ads in the middle of the funnel. You don't need to spend nearly as much on the middle of your funnel, because there will be significantly fewer people in your middle of the funnel audience. Your top of the funnel audience will have over 200,000 people, and the middle will have fewer than 5,000 people. Fewer people in the middle means less ad spend for that audience. **Remember that the middle of your funnel is only for retargeting ads for people who have already engaged with you at the top of the funnel level.**

It gets real once you start spending dollars! Don't worry though, it's all going to be worth it!

SET YOUR BUDGET.

HOW MUCH MONEY SHOULD WE SPEND ON SOCIAL MEDIA ADS?

Most churches are not chomping at the bit to spend money on marketing. In fact, a lack of budget is the primary reason people don't run ad campaigns. I get it. But marketing is a must, and once you start seeing steady growth with your funnel, you will realize that it was worth the investment.

But how much should you be spending? Most people aren't thinking the right way about a marketing budget. When I have the budget talk with church leaders, most of the time they tell me a figure like, "We want to spend $700 for our VBS this year," or something like that. They give me a flat figure for that specific event. That is a good start. Dedicating a separate marketing budget for special events is important, but that isn't how the funnel works. **The funnel is ongoing and never stops.** You need to set aside a recurring monthly budget for your funnel marketing. It is not a one-time figure; it is ongoing. Your funnel budget is a dedicated amount that you spend every single month.

Now that we've got that settled, how much should you spend each month? I fully understand that every church has different budget limitations, so these figures are suggestions based on the marketing campaigns we have set up for hundreds of churches of various sizes. Below is a list of suggested monthly advertising budgets broken down by church size:

$300/month: 0-100 member church
$500/month: 100-500 member church
$750/month: 500-1,000 member church
$1,500/month: 1,000-1,500 member church
$2,000/month: 1,500+ member church

Some of you just lost your mind reading those numbers. You think I'm nuts! I get that. So, for those of you who just fell out of your chairs, please stay with me. Some of you reading this book might actually be spending more than these amounts already, and you think I'm under budget. But if your ads are done according to the funnel systems laid out in this book, you will be able to stay right in this budget range and receive great results. So there, I just saved you money! But whether you think this budget is too much or not enough, here is the news that is really going to make some of you mad at me—and feel free to throw this book against the wall after you read this—this budget is only for social media ads. This does not include Google Ads. Google Ads are a part of the top of the funnel strategy, and we will be diving more into that later in this book.

Once you have accepted the monthly budget, you need to make sure that you spread it correctly between the top and middle of the funnel. The top of your funnel should receive 80% of your budget. The remaining 20% is dedicated for retargeting ads in the middle of the funnel. You don't need to spend nearly as much on the middle of your funnel, because there will be significantly fewer people in your middle of the funnel audience. Your top of the funnel audience will have over 200,000 people, and the middle will have fewer than 5,000 people. Fewer people in the middle means less ad spend for that audience. **Remember that the middle of your funnel is only for retargeting ads for people who have already engaged with you at the top of the funnel level.**

It gets real once you start spending dollars! Don't worry though, it's all going to be worth it!

10 TERMS YOU HAVE TO KNOW.

HOW AM I EVER GOING TO LEARN WHAT ALL THESE SETTINGS MEAN?

Before you can dive deep into your first ad, you first have to learn the terms. There are so many more terms and options with Facebook ads that we could explore, but the ones we discuss here are the most important ones to know. We will do a brief overview of these terms, then we will explore them more in depth when we go through the process step by step.

1. Boosted Posts vs. Traditional Ads

When people tell me that they run Facebook or Instagram ads for their church, 90% of the time that means that they just hit "boost post" on one of their posts. I'm always a supporter of running ads, but this is not how you should do it anymore. The "boost post" feature has very limited options compared to traditional ads. When you learn to set up your ads funnel within Facebook Business Manager, you will be able to have way more control over your ads, such as custom audiences and ad placement, all of which we will discuss more later. This control will allow you to spend your marketing dollars more wisely, so traditional ads are the way to go.

Pro Tip - From now on, when you run ads on Instagram or Facebook you should only use Facebook Business Manager. This will give you much more control of your ads, and you can also give multiple team members access to your ads for collaboration purposes.

2. Facebook Business Manager

Most organizations have multiple people who need to access your page, and Facebook Business Manager is a centralized place for your whole team to administrate your marketing activity. It is a place for businesses to run all aspects of their professional Instagram and Facebook pages. If you have not yet opened a Facebook Business Manager account, you will need to do so before proceeding with this book. Otherwise the rest of this chapter won't make sense. Each step-by-step instruction that I give you in this book references the process for managing ads on Facebook Business Manager.

Pro Tip - To set up your Facebook Business Manager account for the first time, go to business.facebook.com and connect your account there. Take a few moments and familiarize yourself with the different buttons and settings on the dashboard. If this is your first time, it will seem like a whole new world, but don't get stressed and pull your hair out. You will get used to it very quickly. This dashboard is where you will do all of your ad management, conversions, tracking…everything happens through Facebook Business Manager.

3. Campaigns and Ad Sets

Now that you have set up your Business Manager account, it's time to create your first ad! Nice work! Soon I'll walk you through the step-by-step process for launching a new ad. For now, let's start by learning about campaigns and ad sets. Facebook (and every other pay per click medium that I know of) operates by having you organize your ads within campaigns and ad sets. It is way easier to manage multiple ad versions when they are grouped this way.

You can imagine a campaign being like a folder on your computer. Inside that folder you will have at least one or two additional folders. Maybe on your desktop you have a folder called "Photos." And inside that folder you have a folder that says "Family Pics," and then another one that says "Vacation Pics," etc. This is how it works with Facebook ads. Your main folder is the campaign, and inside the campaign are subfolders that are called ad sets. Inside each of those ad set folders are your actual ads.

Here is a great example. Pretend that you are running an ad to invite people to an upcoming worship event at your church. You might call this campaign "Worship Night Promotion." Inside of this Worship Night Promotion campaign, you have two different ad sets. Multiple ad sets allow you to have a different group of ads for different locations. In our example, one ad set is called "Instagram Worship Night Ads" and the other is called "Facebook Worship Night Ads." Inside each of those ad sets are the different ads for your event. It really is just an organization system. Ad sets are simply what they sound like—a "set" or group of ads.

Pro Tip - Arranging your audience, budget, and schedule are usually done in the ad set settings.

4. Campaign Objectives

Once you have wrapped your mind around campaigns and ad sets, it's time to set your campaign objective. Selecting the right campaign objective is one of the most important parts of the Instagram and Facebook ad creation process. Essentially, the campaign objective is the goal for the ad. Is the goal to get more Likes on Facebook? Is the goal of the ad to get people to watch a certain video? How about getting people to visit your website, is that the goal? These are all options for types of campaign objectives.

Pro Tip - Why does this matter so much? It's because the settings and options for your ad are totally different depending on what your campaign objective is. The best campaign objective to use for the top of the funnel is called "Engagement," because it promotes interaction with your content. The best campaign objective to use for your middle of the funnel is "Conversion," because it allows you to track when someone takes action on your website or ads.

5. Custom Audiences

The people to whom your ads are shown are called your audience. Once you create an audience for your ads, you can save it to your list of custom audiences. This is an important step because you want to always focus on the right people with your ads, and saving a custom audience saves you work in the long run.

You can set up an audience based on people's location, age, gender, and online behaviors. If we are honest, it can get downright creepy how much data Facebook has on people. You can even select your audience by their income, or how old their kids are, or what kind of music they listen to. The options are endless.

Pro Tip - When setting up a top of the funnel audience, you may not want to select too many options in the Detailed Targeting section. If you add too many audience filters, you will eliminate thousands of people from seeing your ads.

6. Placements

There are over thirty different options for where your ads can be shown. You can run an ad to be shown on the side of the Facebook page or as a normal post in your feed. You could even place it as an ad in the Instagram stories. This setting is called the placement setting. By default, Facebook has the placement set to "Automatic Placements," which I strongly do not recommend using. **Never use the Automatic Placements setting for an ad.** It will show your ad in all the wrong places.

Pro Tip - Have one ad set dedicated only to Facebook news feed and story placements, and have a separate ad set dedicated to Instagram news feed and story placements. Don't let there be any placements other than news feed or stories. And always separate the Facebook ads from the Instagram ads. This way you can tailor the image size and copy to fit Facebook or Instagram better.

7. Dark Post Ads

When people boost a post, they are simply taking one of the posts on their feed and making more people see it. But what happens when you want to run an ad, but you don't want it to be on your main Instagram or Facebook feed? For this, we use dark posts. These are ads that people in the target audience see like they would any other post but they don't actually appear on the main feed of the church's Facebook or Instagram page. The majority of the ads we run for churches are not actually posts on the main feed, but they are just dark post ads.

Pro Tip - Most of the ads that you run in phase two of your funnel should be dark posts, because they are clear calls to action. With the funnel, you want to only send your ask ads to specific people who have already engaged with the top of the funnel ads. That's why it is important to use dark posts, so only the right people see those ads.

8. Pixel

The way that Facebook ads track when someone visits your website is with a tool called the Facebook pixel. This is a short snippet of web code that you install into your website, which notes when someone has visited your site from your social media.

Pro Tip - Why do we need to set up this pixel? For the funnel to work, we need to show middle of the funnel ads to people who first checked out your website. If someone visits your website with the pixel code installed, they will instantly be added to your retargeting audience. They could literally be on your church's website, and then see your middle of the funnel ads within minutes. That's why this is important.

9. Conversions

When your Facebook or Instagram funnel works, you get a conversion. Remember, we're not talking about someone finding Jesus. It is a marketing term for when someone takes an action on your website. If I was selling T-shirts on my website, a conversion would be when someone completes a purchase online. You set up your conversions in Business Manager for whatever actions you are wanting people to take at the completion of your funnel.

Pro Tip - How does this work for your church? It's all about the Plan Your Visit page in your funnel. Set it up so people are redirected to a Thank You page when they fill out the Plan Your Visit form on your site. Make that Thank You page a conversion event on Facebook Ads Manager. Now when you run a middle of the funnel retargeting ad and someone completes the process, you will see that you have had a conversion. It really isn't that complicated once you set it up for the first time, and you will have real numbers to work with to see how your ads are preforming.

10. Impressions, Reach, and Frequency

If you are a data junky like me, you will love to analyze your ads, and Facebook Business Manager shows you incredible data on their performances. Once an ad has been running for a while, open your Ads Manager and check out the stats. Here you can analyze the behavior and results of each of your ads. The following terms are important to know when analyzing your ads:

Impressions refers to how many times your ad has been shown to anyone. Even if one person sees your ad five times in one day, that still counts as five impressions.

Reach refers to how many people have seen your ad. So if one person sees your ad five times in one day, that only counts as one person reached.

Frequency is the average number of times that one person is seeing your ad. So if your ad is being shown to a person frequently, you will see a frequency of five or six or even higher. If your ad is not being shown very often, you will have a frequency around one.

Pro Tip - When it comes to retargeting ads in the middle of your funnel, you want people to see your ads no more than seven times total. After they have seen it more than seven times, it starts to lose its effectiveness. However, people usually don't respond to an ad until they have seen it at least five to seven times, so this is the sweet spot you want to reach for.

STEP-BY-STEP TRAINING.

CAN SOMEONE PLEASE WALK ME THROUGH THIS THE FIRST TIME?

Of course I'll walk you through it! In this section, I'm going to take you on a step-by-step journey to set up your ad campaigns. For this to make sense, you are going to need to be in front of your computer. If you aren't ready for this, go ahead and skip this section and come back to it later.

Utilizing your Facebook and Instagram marketing funnel isn't hard, except when setting it up for the first time. But once you get the hang of it, and you understand the terms and structure, you will feel much more comfortable with the process. Eventually you will be able to set up an ad campaign in just thirty minutes or less. But like anything new, sometimes the first few run-throughs can be a bit intimidating. No worries though, because I am going to walk you through every step of the process. If you really want to understand this, follow along and actually set up an ad campaign as you read. This way you will really learn it.

In this training, I am going to assume that you have already set up your Facebook Business Manager account, including setting up your ad account. All of these instructions are referencing the process within Facebook Business Manager, not through a personal ads manager. Also keep in mind that the exact names of buttons and links may have changed slightly by the time you read this book. Use your best judgment along the way.

Here we go!

Step 1 - Set up your Top of the Funnel Campaign.

Setting up your campaign for the top of the funnel is where you should start. In Facebook Business Manager, click over to Ads Manager. Once you are there, hit the button that says Create, or Create Ad. If given the option, choose to create a Complete Campaign and not a Campaign Shell. This opens the window where you choose what your Campaign Objective is. If you don't see an image that looks like the image below, please switch to Guided Creation.

Create New Campaign ⓘ	Use Existing Campaign ⓘ	
Campaign: Choose your objective.		Switch to Quick Creation

🏛 **Special Ad Category** ⓘ   Help: Choosing a Special Ad Category

☐ I'm creating a campaign for ads in a Special Ad Category.
Ads related to credit, employment or housing.

What's your marketing objective? Help: Choosing an Objective

Awareness	Consideration	Conversion
Brand awareness	Traffic	Conversions
Reach	Engagement	Catalog sales
	App installs	Store traffic
	Video views	
	Lead generation	
	Messages	

Within the Consideration column, select Engagement. Then scroll down on that same page and make sure the Post Engagement tab is selected. Make sure the toggle button for Create Split Test or A/B Test is toggled to off. Then turn on the toggle button for Campaign Budget Optimization. Campaign budget optimization means that you choose the total budget for this campaign, instead of choosing the budget separately for each ad set. It is just easier this way.

Go ahead and enter your budget. You will have the option to set it as a Daily Budget or a Lifetime Budget. For this ad, let's do a Daily Budget. This means that there is no start/end date to the campaign. It is just an ongoing campaign that spends your budget each day. Don't worry, you can turn the campaign off later or change the budget amounts if you ever want to. Enter the amount that you want to spend each day, depending on what your marketing budget is. Remember, this is the top of the funnel campaign. Our suggestion is to spend 80% of your marketing budget on this campaign. Once you have entered your budget, keep the Campaign Bid Strategy set to Lowest Cost. Set the Campaign Name to "Top of the Funnel Outreach Ads" and then hit Continue.

Step 2 - Create your Ad Set.

The Ad Set page is where we set up our audiences and placements. Now that you are on the Ad Set page, step one is to name this first Ad Set. You are going to be setting up two different Ad Sets. One is only for Facebook ads, and the other is just for Instagram. For now let's go through the process for the Facebook Ad Sets. Later you can go back to set up the Instagram Ad Group by following the same steps, only changing it to Instagram.

On the Ad Sets page, put in the title "Facebook Top of the Funnel Ads." Then the first section is where you set up your

Audience. Select Create New Audience, and we will set up your main top of the funnel audience.

In the Locations section, click Edit and change the option from "Everyone in this location" to "People living in this location." Deselect all preset location options, and an interactive map will appear. Above the map, type in the physical address of your church. Change the radius to be a ten-mile radius. Remember, the purpose of this tutorial is for you to learn the steps. Later you can go tweak these settings to best fit your church.

In the Age section, change it to 18 - 55. Based on our experience, this age range has proven most effective in the top of the funnel. Select All for the genders, and set English as your primary language. You may have to click More Options in order to select your language. Again, you can go back and change these to fit your church later.

Leave the Detailed Targeting section blank. In the top of the funnel, we don't want to filter people based on their interests or demographics. We want to reach everyone in our area. Under the Connections section, change the drop down from "Add Connection Type" to be "Friends of people who like your Page." Go ahead and set it to your church's Facebook page. This is our audience that focuses in on people who are already friends of someone who Likes your page on Facebook. This is an awesome audience for the top of the funnel, because the people are already connected to the church through a friend. See the image below and make sure your settings look the same.

SECRET NINE

GOOGLE MARKETING.

GOOGLE MARKETING.

WHERE DOES GOOGLE MARKETING FIT IN THE FUNNEL?

Everybody loves social media ads, but they don't usually share the love with Google Ads. Google is like the nerdy kid in high school that nobody understands and most people avoid. **Then later in life, they become your boss.**

Many church leaders don't understand what to do with Google. Some churches avoid Google marketing and do nothing with it, while other churches are overly obsessed with Google marketing. They think that it should be the catalyst for their whole marketing strategy. Which route is the best approach? To be honest, the truth lies somewhere in the middle.

Google marketing is a big part of your funnel. It is an incredibly valuable tool. In this chapter, we discuss Search Engine Optimization (SEO), YouTube, Google Ads, the Google Ad Grant, and more. But I have some great news for you! Because you have already learned the structure of Facebook ad campaigns, ad sets, and individual ads, understanding Google Ads will be much easier for you. Google uses the same basic layout for their ad system, so you won't be learning this from scratch.

Google marketing is such an important piece in the puzzle. When someone sees your church on Google, it's because they were looking. On Facebook and Instagram marketing, we don't know if the individual seeing our ads is currently looking for a church or a life change, but with Google, your website is shown to people who are actively searching for things like "churches near me."

In secular marketing, salespeople talk about the different types of "leads" when they are hunting for customers. When a salesperson contacts someone who is not necessarily even interested, they are called a "cold lead." Those cold leads are the least valuable, because the success rate is low. But when a person has already shown signs of purchasing, they are considered a "warm lead." Warm leads are what people want, because they have a much higher success rate. Salespeople are trained to give first priority to the warm leads, since they are most likely to convert to a sale. The principle is similar with Google marketing for your church. People that you reach with Google marketing are like warm leads. They have shown interest in your church based on the terms they are searching online. So if you don't put any marketing budget into Google, you are missing out on all of the warm leads.

I know, I know. It feels weird to refer to people searching for a church as a "lead," but it's just the term! The principle is what you need to understand.

Google is for the top of the funnel. It isn't likely that a person will come to a Sunday service just because they found your website on Google. **Remember, it usually takes seven impressions before someone takes action.** Even if they don't convert during their first visit to your website, that's totally ok, because we have a funnel. Since you have set up your tracking pixel on your website, once this person opens their Instagram or Facebook, they will see your middle of the funnel ads. They will see them over and over until you reach at least seven impressions. This is how it works! There are plenty of ways that someone enters the top of the funnel, and Google is a big player.

Google is a crucial part of your marketing funnel, so don't ignore it just because it is confusing.

GETTING SEO RIGHT.

WHAT IS ALL THIS SEO STUFF REALLY ABOUT?

Google is a great way to get your website in front of the people who are actively looking for a church. There are two ways to use Google for marketing: paid campaigns on Google Ads and organic search results. Organic search results are when your website appears in Google searches without having to pay for it. It is a normal search result. Later in this chapter we are going to talk about paid Google Ads, but first, we should discuss how you can maximize your organic exposure on Google by improving your search engine optimization (SEO).

When your website has poor SEO, it won't show up very highly on results for generic searches like "church in my city." In fact, some churches with very poor SEO won't even rank highly in the results when searching the actual name of their church. That's pretty bad. **A church with great SEO will show up for broad terms that relate to anyone looking for a church in their area.** That is the goal.

Google's search results are based on location, so when someone searches for "church near me" in Tampa, Florida, they will get local results. You definitely want a piece of that action. Google has a complex and ever-changing algorithm for determining which websites should run on the top of their search results list. As professional marketers, we are not given the specific details of their algorithm, but we know the SEO foundations that will improve your church's rank in the generic results. If you make these foundational updates on your website, you will start to rank more highly on the search list.

In marketing, the term SEO is used interchangeably for two different services. Some marketing agencies think of SEO as how your website is initially built. They analyze your site to make sure the proper keywords are used throughout your entire website. They make sure it is indexed properly with Google, as well as a lot of other things like reviewing meta tags, keyword density, and media file names. To other agencies, SEO refers more to the work that you can do after a website is already live to improve the search rankings. For example, we know that Google loves it when you have other high-quality websites linking back to your main website. So SEO agencies will often set up blogs, publications, and other websites to frequently write content that links back to your website. **This is a lot of work, but it does improve rankings.**

Explaining this takes me back to one of the secular marketing campaigns that my team managed. We were working on the marketing funnel for a big real estate company in Los Angeles. After we set up the real estate company's primary website, we actually then went and built a whole other website that was all about the different luxury communities and housing developments in their area. It was a place that featured more than just real estate, but was a resource for people to know the local neighborhoods. We would write weekly blogs and articles on the site, with real estate as a main topic, and we would link back to the primary website for the real estate company whenever possible. Over the next year we became one of the top search results, beating most of their competitors. It was great!

Although this practice is effective in the long run, the primary thing we will be focusing on in this chapter is setting up your website properly for great SEO from the onset. Running a second website is probably too much work for most churches.

How do you know if your website is set up with good SEO? There are a couple of tools that you are going to want to learn that help you analyze your site. The first one is a tool called Google Search Console. To set up your Google Search Console account, you need to…you guessed it…do a Google search for "Google Search Console." This is a free SEO tool from Google that shows you how your website ranks for the local searches that you are focused on. You can type in any search term, and it will instantly show you what number your site is ranked as in the search results. As you go through the setup process with Search Console, it will ask you to install the Google tracking code on your website. You will want to install this code just like you did the Facebook pixel.

Once you have your Google Search Console totally set up, you will have all the data that you need on the SEO performance of your website. You can now see where Google ranks you for specific and broad search terms. With Google Search Console you can also test your website's load speed on both mobile and desktop. Knowing your load speed will help you see what areas are most lacking in your website. If your website takes more than three seconds to load, people won't stick around to wait. You need to improve your load speed by using caching, changing servers, and/or reducing the media file sizes.

Now that you know you need to improve your SEO, what can you do about it? **First, you need to add the exact search terms**

that you want to rank for in the verbiage and text copy of your website. Wherever and whenever, as long as it flows naturally. Here is an example: if you wanted to rank for the search term **"church in Nashville"** then you would change the spot on your website that says "Are you ready to visit us this Sunday?" to say "Are you looking for a **church in Nashville?"**

Whenever you can, adjust your text to have the exact search terms (keywords) that you want to rank more highly for. Take an afternoon and comb through each page on your website and make these changes everywhere you can. Just be careful not to use the same search terms over and over so that it no longer seems natural. In the past, people have tried to game the system and overload a website with repetitive keywords. Google is savvy to that now, and it will penalize your rankings if you do that.

But wait, there is more that you can do! **The next step is to change the title and the alt text on all media on your site.** Most people don't realize that the actual file names for your photos and videos play a big role in Google rankings. There are so many wasted titles on images like "image_homepage.png." That image title should have a keyword in it. Go to each image and video on your website and rename it to one of your focus keywords. Change your files to "church _in_nashville.png" or something like that throughout your site. Trust me, it really helps!

We're still not done yet! On all reputable website builders, there is another spot where you can add additional description words to your photos and videos. They are called alt tags. You should see an option next to every photo you put on your website to add alt tags, or alternate description. Most churches leave this blank because they don't understand what it is. However, Google uses the alt tags to get more info on what your website is all about. You need to make sure every alt tag is filled with strategic keywords. Switch it up with every photo and video, and keep it as natural sounding as possible.

And finally, one of the most important things you can do to improve your search rankings is to update your website regularly. Google wants their users to see the most relevant websites, and they give preference to sites that are updated frequently. Make it a practice to add your message, upcoming events, or even a blog that you update every week. You will start to see your website shoot higher and higher in the search results. **It is a long game, so don't get discouraged if nothing changes in the first few months. Sometimes it takes six months to start seeing results.**

Now that you're familiar with the Google Search Console, the next tool you should sign up for is called Google Analytics. This is another free program from Google, and it is insanely helpful, but also extremely complicated. People even take college classes on this program, so you are going to feel a little overwhelmed with all of the features. Don't worry, you won't use 95% of the features that Google Analytics has, but there are some very useful tools that you need.

One of my favorite tools on Google Analytics is where you can track the most common map that someone follows on your website. This means you can see the order in which people view your pages when they visit your site. This is important so you can know if your pages are pointing people where you want them to go. It will show you how most people land on your home page, and then click to the About page, and then from there to the Messages page…or whatever it is for you. It also lets you see what pages people don't stay on very long, so maybe you can improve the content on those pages. As an example, perhaps you want people to go from the I'm New page to the Plan Your Visit page, but you see that everyone who goes to the I'm New page is only on that page for an average of ten seconds, meaning they aren't staying long enough to see your call to action. You might want to change the layout, copy, and images of your I'm New page so people stay engaged long enough to see and respond to your call to action to visit the Plan Your Visit page.

Google Analytics will also give you info on where people are visiting your site from. Are they on a mobile device or a desktop? Are they close by, or farther away than you expected? This kind of information can really prove helpful as you think about bettering your website experience. If you notice that a huge percentage of your traffic comes from a neighboring city, you might consider doing a blog post about what God is doing in that city, or you might start thinking about opening a campus there. Knowing this information helps you make wise decisions for your church.

Pro Tip - If you are like many churches who have been approached by a business, or offered an SEO management upgrade by a website developer, beware. Agencies will take advantage of people's lack of understanding about SEO and charge them for doing literally nothing. They will throw around terms like "metadata" and "indexing" that you won't understand. You will feel like what they are saying is important, and you'll agree to it. Ninety percent of the time it is a waste of money. If you are going to pay a reputable agency to do your SEO, it should cost well over $1,000 per month. A red flag is when someone offers to do your SEO for something like $200 per month, because they are likely going to do nothing but take your money.

GOOGLE BUSINESS PROFILE.

DO I HAVE TO SET UP A GOOGLE BUSINESS PROFILE?

For your church to have great SEO results, you definitely need to set up your Google Business Profile. What is a Google Business Profile? When you do a Google search for a business or organization in your town, you will see a list of results. Many will just be typical text-only results, with a headline and a description. You will also see some results listed on a map, but you will also see bigger results of organizations with Google Business Profiles set up. They will have a much larger display of information including photos, business hours, reviews, and button-style links to specific pages on their websites. As a church, you want to make sure this is how you show up. When your Google Business Profile is set up, you will get incredibly better results from Google marketing. Take a look at the image below as an example of what business profiles look like.

To set up your Google Business Profile, start by doing a Google search for "set up my Google Business Profile" and click on the first result. Google makes all of its services pop up as the first result, so they are easy to find. Once you click on that link, Google will walk you through each step in the process to set

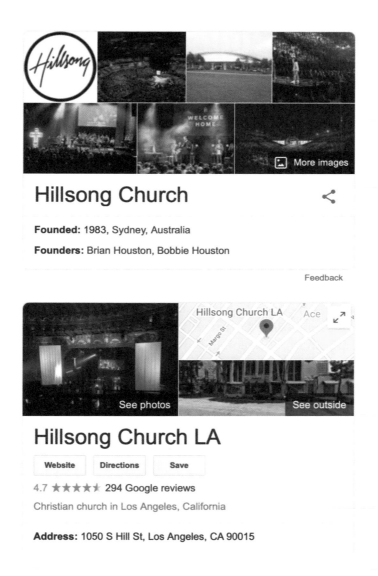

Hillsong Church

Founded: 1983, Sydney, Australia

Founders: Brian Houston, Bobbie Houston

Feedback

Hillsong Church LA

| Website | Directions | Save |

4.7 ★★★★★ 294 Google reviews

Christian church in Los Angeles, California

Address: 1050 S Hill St, Los Angeles, CA 90015

up your profile for the first time. To confirm your address, they will have to call the main phone line or mail a postcard to your church. That is all normal and part of the process.

For many of you, there will already be an existing Google Business Profile that has not been updated or touched in years. This is the most common situation for churches that aren't brand new. In this case, you need to log in to your current Google Business Profile and spruce it up a bit. Add great recent photos, a description of your church, your hours, and anything else that is missing. As Google updates their settings and features for Google Business Profile, take advantage of any additional content you can post about your church. Just make it a practice to log in once a month and make minor improvements.

If you don't know the email address and password for the original Google Business Profile that was set up, there is a process called "Claiming Your Business Profile." This is a button where you can take over administrative rights to a Google Business Profile. Just do a Google search for it and follow the steps to verify that you are in fact an approved administrator for that organization.

Although it is easy to forget about your Google Business Profile, keep in mind that literally hundreds of people see it every single month. Keeping it updated is vital.

whelmed by it.

The second type of person is usually someone on staff who is highly into numbers and data and more of an analytical type of person. They might even wear a pocket protector and thick glasses. But I digress. This person will likely have taken the church all in on Google Ads because it works well with their data-driven brain. They will probably have much less enthusiasm for social media ads, because they are not as clear cut as Google Ads are.

Recently I worked with a church in New Jersey that was heavily using Google Ads. They were spending literally 100% of their marketing budget exclusively on Google. And this wasn't a small budget; they were actually spending over $10,000 per month! This blew my mind when I first looked at their numbers. They were running all kinds of Plan Your Visit ads, and they were getting results with them. **Google Ads are really good, but you can get ten times more results for your budget when they are used within the funnel.** So we changed this church's plan to now spend only a fraction of that $10,000 per month budget on Google Ads. We paired them with social media ads that were top of the funnel ads, then our conversions happened by showing retargeting ads in the middle of the funnel. The church staff immediately started seeing the retargeting ads that we set up all over Instagram and Facebook, and so did their community. Their funnel began producing new visitors on a regular basis much better than their Google Ads had before.

You can see from this story that using Google Ads alone could be successful in marketing a church. You would have to spend a lot on them, but they could produce some results by themselves. On the flip side, a social media ad campaign could work without any Google Ads, too. **But if you put them together in this funnel, you will see long-term results like you never have before.** ⬅

If you have not already set up your own Google Ads account, that is the first step. Just do a Google search for "Google Ads" and follow the setup instructions. Once you have finished the setup, you will be taken to your Google Ads dashboard. It will take you some time to poke around and get familiar with it, but soon you will start to recognize the ad structure. It is the same as Facebook ads. Google Ads also organizes ads with the Campaigns - Ad Groups - Ads format, just like Facebook, so because we already went over this structure in the Facebook ads chapter, I won't re-explain that part to you.

In our experience working with churches, we have learned that there are two main types of Google searches that you should be targeting. The first is location-based searches. You should have a campaign titled "Location Searches," and utilize keywords related to your local area.

A great example of a location-based campaign is an Ad Group with keywords about your city or area, like "churches in Denver" and "church near me" and "best churches in Denver," or anything else that you can think of that people might search for as they look for a church in your city. Once you have all of the keywords selected, **you should always make three or four different ads within each ad group.** You will be able to tell after a few weeks which ad gets the best results, then you can turn the other ones off.

The second type of Google search you should target is the general church search. This is for people who search for specific types of churches, like Baptist or non-denominational churches. Remember that Google Ads are based on the user's physical location, so you do not have to worry about your ads showing up for people outside of your area as long as you set up your location in your ad settings. This campaign should be titled "General Type Searches" and you should choose keywords like "non-denominational churches" and "Baptist churches near me" and "charismatic churches in Denver," or whatever is appropriate for your church. Every month people will be moving to your area who are looking for a church. They are going to hop on Google to search for one, and this campaign is how you reach those people. Beyond just using denominational descriptions, you should also use adjectives like "contemporary church" and "modern church" and "family-friendly churches."

You will notice that I do not suggest running ministry-specific ad campaigns such as "women's ministry" or "men's Bible study." Although you will be able to generate some clicks from those keywords, they are not usually high quality clicks. Because Google Ads are a tool for the top of your funnel, you should dedicate your marketing specifically for people who are searching for a church.

When you are setting up your keywords, you should first do a Google search for "Google Keyword Planner Tool." This is a free tool that Google gives to show you how many people in your area are searching for those keywords. This gives great insight into how many people are actively searching for a church in your area, and the numbers might surprise you!

When you are finishing setting up your ads, you will have an option to add "callout" links. These are four sub links under your ad's main headline, and you should definitely use them. **You get four more links, and it doesn't cost anything extra.** They make your ad way more noticeable, and you have additional space to get your message across. I suggest making at least one of your callout links either Plan Your Visit or My First Time, which will point directly to your I'm New page on your website. Messages, About Us, and Our Mission are other callout links that have proven successful. In the image below, you will see an example of four callout links. In this example, Upcoming Events, Active

Kids, Listen Online, and Plan A Visit are the call out links of choice. You have room to pick and choose which links you think are most important, but always remember what your main call to action is—getting people to plan a visit.

We haven't talked yet about your budget. With Google Ads, you can choose to set your own bid. This bid is how much you are willing to spend for one person to click on your ad. You can set a manual bid, or have Google automatically set it for you. If you are new to Google, I suggest letting Google set it for you using its automated bidding feature. This means that you tell Google what you are willing to spend per day, and Google will automatically take care of the ad bidding. For areas where there are many businesses bidding for the same keywords, the businesses with a lower bid will have their ad shown less often and lower on the results page. If you want to really be success- ful with Google Ads, you need to spend more per bid so that your result is on the top of the page. The top results get way more clicks, so it is worth the extra cost.

I suggest starting out on Google Ads with a $10 per day budget if you are a smaller church, and as you grow, you should increase your daily budget proportionately. Even if you are a large ministry, I would tap your Google Ads budget out at $50 per day. That is sufficient for most large urban areas. Any budget over $50 per day should be put back into social media. Your social media ads will always represent at least 80% of the volume in the top of your funnel.

Besides budget, Google also uses a metric called click through rate (CTR) to determine your ad's placement order. It isn't as simple as paying more to get the top result, because your ad has to get a lot of clicks to make the top of the list. A good benchmark is an 8%-10% click through rate. If you have an ad or a keyword that is getting way less than 8% CTR, you should adjust the ad and keywords until it performs better.

Pro Tip - I have found after years of managing Google Ads for churches that cute ad copy just does not work. The first line of your Google Ad should simply be the church name. Don't start with a description or a cool one-liner. It just does not perform as well as when you start with the church name. A solid ad headline is something like "New Life Church | Christian Church in Raleigh, NC." I know it isn't fancy, but it works.

GOOGLE AD GRANTS.

I HEARD ABOUT A $10,000/MONTH FREE ADS PROGRAM.
HOW DO I GET ME SOME OF THAT?

If you haven't heard of the Google Ad Grant program, let me give you the inside scoop. Google has a program specifically for nonprofits. It allows you to run Google Ads at no cost at all to you, up to $10,000 per month. Pretty awesome! They don't give you cash, so don't get too excited, but it is a monthly credit for Google Ads. This is a big deal for churches who are jumping into this whole paid marketing world for the first time. As a new church, budget can certainly be an issue!

You must be thinking, $10,000 per month in free advertising?! This is the greatest thing ever! It really is a great thing, and you need to set it up for your church. But it isn't quite as amazing as it sounds. Let me explain.

When Google Ad Grants first came out, it was hugely impactful for churches. We would run ad campaigns for churches and get hundreds of clicks per month, and it was amazing. However, now that the word has gotten out, it is an oversaturated market. With the Google Ad Grant program, there are some rules and limitations. One of the limitations is that you are capped at a $2 bid per ad, which makes it almost impossible to spend anywhere near the $10,000 monthly allowance. However, there is a way to remove the $2 bid cap. If you use the automated bidding option, and you can consistently keep all of your keywords and ads performing at a 5% or better CTR, then Google Ad Grants will lift the $2 per bid cap. The problem is that it is very easy to dip below 5% on many generic search terms.

It is difficult to gain the maximum potential of the Google Ad Grant. But not impossible. By the time you are reading this book, the Google Ad Grant requirements will possibly have adjusted these metrics, and you should find out what the rules and limitations are at the current moment.

But right now, here's how the oversaturated market affects churches: with so many churches using the Google Ad Grant program, everyone is competing for the same keywords. And everyone has the same bidding limitations, so each church is essentially bidding the same amount for their ads. This means that your church's ads won't get shown as frequently as you need, so it becomes much less impactful for your funnel.

So what is the work around? Smart churches have gone back to running traditional Google Ads and actually paying for them, instead of using the Google Ad Grant program. Why would they do that when it is free? It's because when you are paying, you are not limited to the bid cap. So you can set your bid at $2.01 per click and beat 95% of the competitors for that keyword. Your ads will trump all the Ad Grant campaigns because you are paying with real money.

This is an incredible opportunity. **The market is oversaturated with Google Ad Grants, but it is very unsaturated with traditional Google Ad spend.** Right now if you maximize and optimize everything possible with the Google Ad Grant program, you will only be able to generate around one hundred to three hundred clicks per month. But if you run traditional ads you will generate ten times those numbers. That is a good use of a marketing budget! The smart Google Ad Grant strategy is to use it, but also use a traditional Google Ads campaign at the same time. Go ahead and set up the Google Ad Grant program, even though your results will be limited. Any time you have an opportunity to get free traffic to the top of your funnel, jump on it. **Just run the traditional ads as well.**

How do you get set up for Google Ad Grants? It's a bit of a process, but totally worth it. The first step is to sign up for Google for Nonprofits. Do a quick Google search for "Google for Nonprofits," and go through their verification process. Google uses a third-party entity called TechSoup to verify your church's nonprofit status. They will ask you to set up a TechSoup account and enter your church's EIN number, address, and a few other details. TechSoup needs to verify that you are a legitimate nonprofit organization.

Once you have submitted all of the required information, it takes two to six weeks for TechSoup to verify your organization. You will get an email from TechSoup after it is complete. The next step is to log back into your Google for Nonprofits account, and you will see that your account has new features! Even a few more features beyond just the Ad Grant program. You will have access to free branded Gmail accounts, Map APIs, and a few other features in the Google for Nonprofits platform.

The next step in the process is to sign up for Google Ads in your Google for Nonprofits account. Before starting, make a brand new Gmail account that you only intend to use for this Google Ad Grant account. This is important. Your Google Ad Grant account cannot be linked to your traditional Google Ads account; they have to be separate. Google's Ad Grant setup process is not as smooth as it could be, and if you make one mistake along the way, you will have to start the process all over again. It's terrible. For example, if you enter your billing info into your Google Ad Grant account, it no longer will be a valid account. Why is this? There is no good reason; it is just a glitch in Google's setup system. A lot of people get stuck in this very spot, so trust me and don't enter your billing information during setup. Just one little mistake makes the whole process have to start over.

Once you have your new Gmail account activated, you are ready to set up your Google Ad Grant account! Move forward with creating your settings and ads like you would a traditional account from here. There are a few more rules you must follow when launching your Google Ad Grant account, or Google will not approve your Ad Grant setup:

1. You are required to have at least two ad groups set up from the beginning.
2. Each ad group must have at least two ads in them.
3. You cannot use any single-word keywords. For example, don't use "church." It needs to be a longer keyword like "church in Nashville."
4. You must not enter your billing info.

After you go through setting everything up, go back to your Google for Nonprofits account. Hit Activate next to Google Ads, and enter the Google Ads account number that you just received. It takes Google around three business days to approve your new Ad Grant account. But after that, you are set!

It would really be a bummer to go through all of these verification steps, only to have your account removed later. This happens if you don't maintain it properly. You must regularly check in on the account, and update it frequently to ensure that your ads are preforming above the 5% CTR minimum. Log in once a week and update your ads, tweak your keywords, and try new ideas. If you let your ad account go dormant, Google will cancel it. Then you have to start this whole thing over again.

It is a process to get approved, but once you do, you will get some free traffic for the top of your funnel!
get your message across. I suggest making at least one of your callout links either Plan Your Visit or My First Time, which will point directly to your I'm New page on your website. Messages, About Us, and Our Mission are other callout links that have proven successful. In the image below, you will see an example of four callout links. In this example, Upcoming Events, Active

SECRET TEN

THE BONUS NUGGETS.

THE BONUS NUGGETS.

WHAT ELSE SHOULD WE DO TO BUILD OUR FUNNEL?

There are so many more topics than we can cover in one book. Marketing and advertising is always changing, so I am sure we will have a follow-up book later at some point. In this chapter we won't go as in-depth on the concepts, but I wanted to share a few more strategies from a high level.

CAN WE TALK ABOUT ONLINE REVIEWS?

Not long ago, my team was studying the web analytics for a church we work with in San Francisco. When we checked the stats for their organic web traffic, we were shocked. They received a ton of traffic from Yelp. Like, a ton. This was eye opening to me. I had not deeply considered that Yelp would play a big factor for a church's marketing. I was wrong! Yelp brought in more than double the traffic of Instagram or Facebook. More than double!

Although this was surprising to us, it totally makes sense. We are in a review-driven culture. Before I personally buy something online, I usually read the reviews. It is just part of how we make online decisions. **Even though choosing a church is not a purchase, it still is a decision.** Your church should make a big deal about getting more reviews—hopefully good ones. It may seem weird to ask for reviews, but they can be a deciding factor in the decision-making process.

Many churches don't want to ask for reviews, because they worry about the negative ones. We all know that people online can be brutal, and sometimes totally inaccurate, but most people are savvy enough to filter through oddball reviews. Even some of the most popular movies, books, and restaurants receive negative reviews. When I am looking for reviews and I read some of the negative ones, I can instantly tell when someone is credible or not. I honestly don't think that your church will be greatly impacted by someone spewing inaccurate and crazy reviews.

What you need is volume. You want as many reviews as possible. It's better to have a 3/5 star rating with tons of reviews, than it is to have a 5/5 star rating, with only three reviews. If you only have a few reviews, people know that those were just from you and your mom! You aren't tricking anyone.

The way to up your review game is pretty simple: you just have to ask. In the secular world, they teach entire classes to marketers about following up and asking for reviews. **When someone is asked, they are way more likely to leave a review.** Find ways to ask your people for a review. Use an occasional Facebook post, or put it in your bulletin. It is much more about the number of reviews than the actual content of each one.

Pro Tip - Put a QR code on the screens before your service. Direct people to a landing page on your website where they can have a direct link to Facebook Reviews, Google Reviews, and Yelp for your church.

WHAT ABOUT PRINT MAIL?

Church leaders ask me every week what my advice is about print mail. It's a tricky one to answer. Print mail is a big pill to swallow because it is so darn expensive. With digital ads, you can expect to pay around $0.03 per impression. With print mail, you will spend $0.40 or greater per piece. That's a really big bill when you start doing 30,000-piece mail campaigns. Ouch. Expect a big print mail campaign to cost anywhere from $20,000 to $50,000, depending on your volume. So yeah, it is expensive. However, you can't argue with the results. Print mail does work to get people in the door, especially if it is done surrounding a big event or has a really great and unique message on it.

I suggest doing two big print mail campaigns per year. One for Easter, and one for your second biggest event each year. You might have a huge fall festival, or you might go all out for Christmas Eve. Whatever your second biggest event is, this should have a mailer as well. Some people respond better to mailers than they do online ads.

Your print mail campaign will be most effective if you are strategic with the image and message. If your special event is a big family event, make the message and visuals directed at kids. Use visuals and verbiage that would make the kids beg their parents to take them! As a parent, I hate myself for even writing that, but it works. Win the kids, win the family. The more specific you can make your postcard, the better.

Pro Tip - Instead of traditional mail companies, use Every Door Direct Mail (EDDM). This is a service provided directly by the USPS.

It is cheaper than going through a third-party print mail company. EDDM puts the mailer in every single mailbox in the postal routes that you select. You don't even have to leave a spot for a return address. This gives you more space to promote your message.

WHAT DO YOU MEAN WHEN YOU TALK ABOUT BIG SUNDAYS?

Your marketing will be way more effective when you use big Sundays as the draw. A "big Sunday" is a service when something special happens—something outside the usual weekend service at your church. This might be as simple as the launch of a new teaching series, and you make a big deal about it. Or it can be an event like your church's annual birthday celebration. Something that gives a person a little FOMO (fear of missing out).

With any middle of the funnel ads, you will see a much better conversion rate when the ask is for a big Sunday. People need a big event to feel like it makes sense to stop by for the first time.

Intentionally make a big Sunday happen every single quarter. Any more than that and it loses its effectiveness. Start promoting and talking about your upcoming big Sunday around five weeks in advance, both online and in service. Build excitement, and encourage your people to invite guests for this specific big Sunday.

Pro Tip - Any time you can have a special party happening for the kids, you will see an overall boost in attendance. Advertise that you are having a special superhero character visiting, or you are doing a bounce house. If the parents are getting begged by their kids, you know you've got a great chance for them to show up.

HOW DO WE PROMOTE OUR MESSAGE SERIES?

Every new sermon series is a big deal. In fact, make it a huge deal. Set a precedent that your church goes all in on sermon series. This way people will get excited when you are about to launch a new one.

Most churches use themed message series, but they really don't do anything special. They may teach on a similar topic, but they could do so much more to build excitement. Increase people's anticipation and expectation by treating your series like the launch of a brand new product. Every series needs a creative main graphic and bumper/promo video. Every week, create quote graphics and recap videos that have the message series designs within them. Have banners created to hang in the foyer of the church that are specific to that series, helping to make it feel like a big deal. People love theming, and it helps them visually remember the content that you teach. **This isn't a gimmick, this is us understanding how the human brain works.**

Here's the best way to promote a new series. When you are two or three weeks away from the launch date, make a Facebook event for the first day of the new series, then share it from your church Facebook page. Use the promo video in the Facebook event. Also film a short, one-minute video of the lead pastor sharing the vision and overview of the series. Use this video as a middle of the funnel retargeting ad in the weeks leading up to this launch. Your call to action should be for people to plan their visit for this new series.

It's also a good idea to have some merch created just for your series. Some people in your church will be really moved by a certain message series, and they will want an apparel item as a reminder. Give away unique invite cards or keepsakes with the theme and main points of the series to really make it stick for people.

Pro Tip - *Create a set of Instagram story highlights specifically for each series. Save all the quotes and caption recaps from the series, that way people can look back months or years after the series is over and be reminded of the great content that they learned.*

LET'S WRAP IT UP.

THIS WAS A LOT TO TAKE IN!

Let's zoom out for a minute. The goal of this book is to teach how marketing works in a structured and strategic funnel, not just an aimless hope for results. I've seen thousands of successful and long-term results using this funnel. **With over a decade of marketing experience, I have not found any better system.**

You might feel overwhelmed by the how-to sections, and I get that. You might need to read them a few more times to really get them, but by the end of this book, you now have a full understanding of what the funnel is. Understanding how to use the funnel is the most important thing you need to know. It is a principle—first things come first. The system of setting up the ads will get easier the more you practice.

I knew when I wrote this book that it will rub some people the wrong way. I intentionally didn't spend time giving a lot of disclaimers about how God is the one who grows a church, and how the church is not a corporation, and how God doesn't need advertising…all that good stuff. Why? Because this book is for church leaders. We already know that God doesn't need any of this to grow his church. But I am so thankful that he uses us, and he lets us be a part of reaching people.

God could grow your church without any marketing at all. Obviously. On the other side of things, you could do all the funnels and marketing campaigns from this book, and still not have a growing church if God isn't in it.

In reality, God does not need every church to be huge. That's not the point. The reason for all this work and effort is because we want to be faithful. **We want to have a desperate urge to reach people in every way possible.** Let's be faithful with the money and time we spend on marketing, so we can make it effective. With this new knowledge, your church doesn't have to waste money on ineffective marketing. Now you know how to do it right.

If God has called your church to reach more people, use this knowledge to do it the right way. Now you will see measurable results. If you want a professional agency to help your church with media, please be sure to consider my agency, which you can find online at VibrantAgency.com.

But whether you get help or do it all on your own, I encourage you to think long term with your funnel. Don't be discouraged in the beginning stages, because it will take time to produce results. When you plant seeds, you don't see the growth that is being produced underground. **So don't focus on results, but be obsessed with progress.** Keep planting new seeds every day, and the fruits will come.

There are people out there, right now, who are ready to hear from you. For whatever reason, they are ready to try church.

This isn't about systems, this is about those people. Use this book to sharpen your skills and improve your understanding. **Then take action.** Some people use the excuse that God will just bring people to your church and grow it if he wants. In reality, these people just don't want to put in the hard work. **Grit and effort are required to be those hands and feet.**

Reaching people takes intentionality.

Reaching people takes excellence.

Reaching people is what we're called to do.

Go and be the best fisher of men that you can be.

With love,
Ross Turner

COPYRI

Products, pictures, trademarks, and trademarked names are used at various spots in this book to describe proprietary products that are owned by third parties. No endorsement whatsoever of the information contained in this book is given by the owners of such products and trademarks, and no endorsement is implied by the inclusion of product, pictures, or trademarks in this book.

The Funnel: 10 Secrets of Extraordinary Church Growth. Copyright 2020 by Ross Turner. All rights reserved under International and Pan-American Copyright Conventions. By payment of the required fees, you have been granted the nonexclusive, nontransferable right to access and read the text of this printed book or e-book. No part of this text may be reproduced, transmitted, downloaded, decompiled, reverse-engineered, or stored in or introduced into any information storage and retrieval system, in any form or by any means, whether electronic or mechanical, now known or hereafter invented, without the express written permission of Salty Publishing Company.

GHT

Products, pictures, trademarks, and trademarked names are used at various spots in this book to describe proprietary products that are owned by third parties. No endorsement whatsoever of the information contained in this book is given by the owners of such products and trademarks, and no endorsement is implied by the inclusion of product, pictures, or trademarks in this book.

All Scripture quotations taken from The Holy Bible, New International Version®, NIV® Copyright © 1973, 1978, 1984, 2011 by Biblica, Inc.® Used by permission. All rights reserved worldwide.

ABOUT THE PUBLISHER.

Salty Publishing Company

www.saltypublishing.com

info@saltypublishing.com

Pismo Beach, California